The Practitioner Inquiry Series

Marilyn Cochran-Smith and Susan L. Lytle, Series Editors

(continued)

ACTING OUT!

Combating Homophobia
Through Teacher Activism

Edited by
Mollie V. Blackburn,
Caroline T. Clark,
Lauren M. Kenney,
and **Jill M. Smith**

Foreword by JoBeth Allen

TEACHERS COLLEGE PRESS

Teachers College, Columbia University
New York and London

Published by Teachers College Press, 1234 Amsterdam Avenue, New York, NY 10027

Library of Congress Cataloging-in-Publication Data

Acting out!: combating homophobia through teacher activism / Mollie V.
    Blackburn . . . [et al].
    p. cm. — (The practitioner inquiry series)
    Includes bibliographical references and index.
    ISBN 978-0-8077-5031-5 (pbk. : alk. paper)
    ISBN 978-0-8077-5032-2 (hardcover : alk. paper)
    1. Homophobia in schools—Prevention. 2. Homophobia in high schools—
Prevention. 3. Sexism in education—Prevention. 4. Sexual minority students—
Violence against. I. Blackburn, Mollie V., 1969–
    LC212.8.A27   2009
    371.826′64—dc22   2009027089

ISBN 978-0-8077-5031-5 (paper)
ISBN 978-0-8077-5032-2 (hardcover)

Printed on acid-free paper
Manufactured in the United States of America

17   16   15   14   13   12   11   10   8   7   6   5   4   3   2   1

In memory of J. F. Buckley,
a founding Pink TIGer
1946–2008

Contents

Foreword

HOW MANY TIMES IN CLASSES, social groups, or relationships—in the daily living of our lives—do we blunder, insult, objectify, marginalize, remain silent, silence others, or assume too much or too little? Sometimes there is no opportunity to repair damaged relationships. The insight comes too late, we do not have enough courage, our colleague/friend/loved one does not have enough faith in us or we in them. But sometimes, maybe more often than we realize, maybe even years later, we can reopen that damaged space and enter into dialogue.

Acting Out! offers readers the shared wisdom of teachers who can open dialogic spaces and perhaps even reopen damaged spaces, as one of its authors did for me.

One of the Pink TIGers is a friend and colleague. I'll call her Felicia, a pseudonym I used in another writing. Many years ago we were in a study group focusing on teaching for social justice. Felicia had moved away, but was visiting on a Saturday when our group met. Another member and I brought the group a short story with a central character who was a lesbian. Heterosexism was an area of social justice that we had not previously discussed, so the timing seemed perfect. Felicia had recently come out as lesbian, although not to the whole group.

The discussion was tense. One member emphatically rejected the place of literature with gay characters in her middle school library, while Felicia argued (pretty much alone) that this attitude excluded a whole group of people who needed to see that there were other people like them in the world. Years later when I asked her about that meeting Felicia reflected, "I left wondering whether you had inadvertently set me up by choosing this story just because I was coming in town and could thus be depended on to do the work of discussing it. Now I can see, if I was set up, so was [the colleague who objected]. She likely had no idea that someone in the group could be so hurt by her words."

We couldn't go back and repair that painful morning, nor erase the damaged feelings that lingered a decade later. But when I opened the wound and asked Felicia to share her feelings (still asking her to do the work), she generously shared not only insights but also strategies for opening dialogic spaces.

Perhaps the group needed time to talk about lesbian and gay people and their concerns without a lesbian or gay person present to get their ideas out there, to take tentative stances, to raise questions, to revise stances. Perhaps I needed someone else who was gay or lesbian, or at least someone who was really practiced at being an ally, in the group to back me in my concerns. Or maybe it needed to go exactly as it went.

When Freire (1970) posited love and faith as a condition of dialogue, he emphasized that it must be a critical, not naïve, faith. My naïveté—what Felicia insightfully identified as my lack of experience in being an ally— and my lack of empathy or love set up the wrong conditions for dialogue. Freire (1998) emphasized that, as educators, we must have an "armed love," the "fighting love of those convinced of the right and the duty to fight, to denounce, and to announce." (p. 41). I was not equipped, and neither was anyone else in the group. My love of Felicia and of the group was a naïve love; we needed a critical or "armed" love, a deeper critical consciousness. I needed the ability to look at the larger context to see how my actions might impact those I loved. In addition, we failed to engage in collaborative critical thinking leading to critical action—the kind that you will read about throughout *Acting Out!*

If you have picked this book up and are an educator who is LGBTQ, or straight but not narrow, or an ally in training, or just curious—yes, that's a starting point—you might have lots of questions. Most of us do, because teacher preparation programs (including those at my university) and professional learning opportunities rarely focus on issues of homophobia and heterosexism. *Acting Out!* provides readers with multiple perspectives and shares engaging and challenging classroom experiences from teachers asking similar questions.

What if your students, your colleagues, or your administrators are resistant to an antihomophobia curriculum? What happens in that overhyped and understudied transition from idealistic college student fighting for social justice to the realistic 1st-year teacher questioning a heteronormative curriculum or sponsoring a gay-straight alliance? What issues do teachers face about coming out, not coming out, being out, or being an ally? How can teachers who are passionate about this work help their students explore LGBTQ issues through critical inquiry, literature, interdisciplinary research, and writing? Are teachers and teacher educators the only ones who can work for social and educational equity for LGBTQ students and families, or can someone in the district office play a meaningful role? How do all of us consider our sexual orientation in relation to our race, gender, social class, religion, and ethnicity? And perhaps most importantly, how can teachers come together across differences to become change agents in our classrooms, our schools, and our communities?

Acting Out!, like most effective religious leaders, both afflicts the comfortable (those who have not examined their heterosexist privilege), and comforts the afflicted (those who have been marginalized, mistreated, even physically threatened because of their sexual orientation or anti-homophobia work). The book is thought-provoking, challenging, educational, and tremendously encouraging. The authors are teachers and teacher educators who are devoting their time and scholarship, their private and public lives, to working together to combat homophobia—generating a dialogue that our society has by and large failed to have. As I write this, Lt. Dan Choi, a West Point graduate with many years of distinguished service, has been dismissed from the United States Army simply for saying that he is gay.

There are other aspects of *Acting Out!* that make it an invaluable resource. The research process is transparent without overshadowing the inquiry itself. I plan to use it as an example of writing up action research with my students. The first-person narratives resound with distinctive voices, yet work in harmony across the text, integrating theoretical grounding, previous research (albeit scant), and most of all detailed practices and their impact on students and teachers in K–12 and university classrooms. The final chapter helps readers contemplate the evolution of individual teachers, as well as the Pink TIGers as a group, in becoming activists in a variety of ways—some which at first they did not even recognize as activism. This thoughtful reflection will help readers feel that they can start wherever they are and take small but meaningful steps in fighting homophobia

And finally, the annotated bibliography is not just another list; it is *useful*. This valuable resource for teachers and teacher educators includes websites, young adult literature, national surveys, teacher education literature, and selections from magazines and other popular media, films, and videos. What is especially helpful about this bibliography is that the authors explain how they used the various texts in their classrooms, in their study group, and in their roles as activists.

Felicia, I'm working hard at becoming a better ally. Thank you and your colleagues for *Acting Out*!

—JoBeth Allen

References

Freire, P. (1970). *Pedagogy of the oppressed.* New York: Continuum.
Freire, P. (1998). *Pedagogy of freedom: Ethics, democracy, and civic courage.* Lanham, MD: Rowman & Littlefield.

Acknowledgments

OUR WORK WAS FUNDED, and became increasingly intense, with a grant from the National Council of Teachers of English (NCTE) Research Foundation through The Ohio State University. This grant supported the purchase of books and films, travel to conferences, and a writing retreat, which served as the foundation for this book. NCTE's funding was integral in helping us to find, share, and develop our individual and collective voices.

Our students, who have sat in our classrooms; had patience with our faltering work as educators and activists; and shared so much via their writings, interviews, and class discussions, are the heart of this book. They motivate us to make schools better for all of them, every day.

Brian Ellerbeck, our Teachers College Press editor, had boundless enthusiasm for and faith in this project from the start, and we are deeply appreciative of his prompt and caring guidance.

Without the input, dedication, and trust of each and every Pink TIGer—both those with chapters here as well as others—this book would not have been possible. Over the years, we have moved from being a group of individual educators who wanted to do more to combat homophobia to a team who did it—and are still doing it with no intention of slowing.

And finally, we are grateful to our loved ones and friends who have driven us to meetings, fed us, and listened with care. These individuals were in many ways just as much a part of the Pink TIGer movement as the TIGers themselves.

Teacher/Activists Who Became Pink TIGers

An Introduction

MOLLIE V. BLACKBURN, CAROLINE T. CLARK,
LAUREN M. KENNEY, AND JILL M. SMITH

A S WE REFLECT ON HOW the Pink TIGers came to be, perhaps it's not surprising that the seeds of our work were sown in the summer of 2004. That was a national election year, and while November was still months away, Ohio lawns were already sprouting political signs in support of either John Kerry or George W. Bush. In addition to experiencing the presidential race, Ohio, like other states, was in the midst of a brewing battle over same-sex marriage. That summer, signatures were being collected to have a constitutional amendment added to the ballot asserting that only a union between one man and one woman would constitute a marriage in the state of Ohio, even though there already existed a state law prohibiting same-sex marriages. This became Issue 1, and its subsequent passage would spawn one of our first activist moves. Even as our group was forming, it was clear that ours was a state where much work was needed to combat homophobia and heterosexism.

Clearly, the time and place of our group matter. Had we started meeting 6 years before we had, our motives may have been grounded in the murder of Matthew Shepard rather than the rejection of same-sex marriages, for example. Had we been living in Massachusetts instead of Ohio, we may have felt more hopeful, less cynical, since that was the year that the Supreme Judicial Court of Massachusetts declared it unconstitutional for only heterosexual couples to be allowed to marry. But it was 2004, and we were in Ohio.

Against this political backdrop, Jim Buckley and Jeane Copenhaver-Johnson, English and education faculty at The Ohio State University (OSU) Mansfield Campus, invited Mollie Blackburn and Caroline Clark, both education faculty at the OSU main campus, to come together to discuss the possibility of running a workshop to teach teachers to use literature with lesbian, gay, bisexual, and transgender (LGBT[1]) themes in their elementary, middle, and high school classrooms. Jim and Mollie were already collaborating on an article arguing for teaching queer-inclusive English language arts (Blackburn & Buckley, 2005), while Jeane and Caroline had each taken steps to address gender and sexuality in their university teaching. All four were experienced English and language arts teachers in K–12 or university settings or both. Mollie, as a lesbian, and Jim, as a gay man, were angry about and frustrated by having their rights and freedoms voted on by others. Caroline and Jeane were, and are, allies. According to the Gay, Lesbian and Straight Education Network (GLSEN), "Allies generally are non-LGBT people who are committed to ending bias and discrimination against LGBT people," but they can be "anyone who supports ending anti-LGBT name-calling, bullying and harassment in schools. For instance, a bisexual adult can be an ally to LGBT students, and a lesbian student can be an ally to a transgender student" (http://www.allyweek.org/about/index.cfm). (This definition suggests that allies are limited to schools; they are not, but schools are the focus of GLSEN and the primary focus of this book.) As straight allies, Caroline and Jeane shared Mollie and Jim's frustration and anger and were seeking ways to work with these colleagues and friends for positive change. Through her prior work with lesbian, gay, bisexual, transgender, and questioning (LGBTQ) youth in community settings, Mollie also knew that these kinds of broader political issues would have consequences for queer and questioning youth in schools. The initiation and passing of Issue 1 might have signaled to young people that bullying and harassment of LGBTQ classmates were acceptable in our state, exacerbating the already homophobic climate of schools (Kosciw, Diaz, & Greytak, 2008). Addressing homophobia and heterosexism in classrooms seemed a way to work for change, and supporting teachers to do this work through LGBT-themed literature in schools tapped the curricular and political experiences and expertise shared by Jim, Jeane, Mollie, and Caroline.

After discussing the kinds of change and impact they sought, the four decided that inviting teachers to meet over time, rather than attend a single workshop, would better suit their aims. Together, they drafted an invitation to teachers who might be interested in doing antihomophobia work in their classrooms, particularly through literature and film, and willing to commit themselves to meeting once a month for 6 months. Jim, Jeane, Mollie, and Caroline sent the invitation via email to K–12 and university teachers whom they thought might be drawn to such a project. An initial meeting was held late that summer, and though at first only a 6-month commitment was requested, that commitment has been renewed repeatedly over time. For more than 4 years, this group has met monthly at members' homes on Saturday mornings. Of the nine people who attended that first meeting, eight have remained as steadfast participants and several new members have joined since. After that first meeting, we developed a regular schedule and an active email list. Beyond our monthly meetings, participants regularly shared news items and updated one another on happenings in our classrooms and communities via email. Email allowed us to remain connected with members who could not attend every meeting and provided a space for us to praise, support, vent, and empathize with one another's efforts. Meeting notes were also shared and amended over email. We mention these details here as a way of offering suggestions of things to do in similarly committed inquiry groups.

Through early fall 2004 we searched for terms to describe ourselves, often opening our email messages with lines like "Hi groupies" and "Hi group." But it was the results of the November 2004 election that pushed us to choose a purposeful name that would stick. For our group, November 3rd was a day for venting and empathy. The state had elected to amend the constitution to prevent same-sex marriages, with more than 61% of voters supporting the change. Our emails from that time capture our feelings of devastation and show how our group developed, even beyond our monthly meetings. Lesley Colabucci, a lesbian colleague teaching on the OSU Mansfield campus, responded to an email from Dana Ogrodwoski, a straight ally teacher in central Ohio and a regular participant in our group, who had asked how the group was feeling the day after the election:

> Late this week I noticed a flyer in support of Issue 1 a few doors down from mine here at Mansfield campus. I remember feeling surprised and almost shocked for some reason. The overwhelming feeling I was left with as I continued to pass that door over and over was concern for the students who have to pass that door or maybe even knock on it. Somehow my thoughts and energy were focused on anonymous, struggling glbt people who might find the support for Issue 1 hurtful and a reminder of their second-class

status and the dangers of being out. It wasn't until I walked by it this morning that I realized I might actually have a real and personal response to it as well. Isn't that strange? It's like I distanced it and thought of it in relation to others but not for me until this morning. Why would I think I was confident or strong enough to not be moved by the support for Issue 1? Just because I've been out for so long? Or used to marginalization and hatred for so long? Or b/c I think so differently about marriage that it wasn't really on my radar? I don't know. . . . I'd love to hear how any of you make sense of my response and how you are thinking and feeling about the passing of Issue 1 (especially any insight on how it definitely will not hold up to constitutional scrutiny!). Thanks for the chance to vent! Lesley

In her reply to Lesley and the group, Lauren Kenney, an out lesbian high school English teacher and regular participant in our group meetings, pushed us to consider a name for ourselves that would capture our shared commitments to equality and justice, as well as our outrage:

it's like being kicked in the stomach. we knew it was going to pass, but still i think we should start an activist group a la the black panthers. the pink panthers. we need to unite—nothing will happen until we're unified—to rise up. i believe that change is happening—ten years ago, perhaps this issue would have won by a much wider margin. now we really need to push. i feel very sad, and overwhelmed, and like we've just regressed 50 years, but i see no option but to work. . . . teaching is a small contribution. it's nice, here—the teachers in my school are enraged and upset right now. i'm so glad i work in this building. to me, it gives our group much more urgency. and work that many of you do with GSAs. it feels like it's not enough, but it's huge. every small thing we do is a step in the right direction. the change is happening.

The day continued with emails expressing sadness, empathy, and outrage. Mollie, as a committed partner and parent, shared her visceral response to the vote on her rights:

I look at my baby daughter and wonder what I've done bringing her into this world where the homophobic public gets to vote on the rights of her parents, whether we get them. It just breaks my heart. So maybe there's hope in the Pink Panthers. What do we do? How do we do it? What does it have to do with teaching? What does it have to do with literature? Everything? Nothing? Glad you are all doing your work in the world. —Mollie

Caroline shared her feelings as a straight mother, someone presumably not affected by this vote:

This whole day breaks my heart. I picked up my daughter from school today, and so many of us were on the brink of tears, or simply crying. . . . It was hard to be surrounded by so many great kids who are so optimistic and to be so worried about the world we're creating for them. I heard some radio voice (an "expert") say that the votes on gay marriage nationwide are signs of progress to come. That being 50/50 on an issue as a nation now is part of all the transitions that have happened in this country—around slavery, integration, civil rights—all of it. The trend, he claims, is good. We're moving forward, not backward. I also heard that these votes are generationally marked—that young people are not the ones voting for these hateful initiatives. I have to hold on to this hope. —Caroline

And Dana responded with a call for an impromptu meeting at her house to discuss ideas for responses and ways to make change. Lauren captured the shift in the group, responding to Dana's invitation, "I will come. I will make time. The other teachers at my school may want to join us." By the end of that day, we had clearly shifted from teacher inquiry to activism. Eventually, we came to call ourselves the Pink TIGers. "Pink" comes from the inverted pink triangle that some LGBT people claim as a symbol, and "TIGers" is an acronym for those who participate in our Teacher Inquiry Group, and it captures the confidence, strength, and at times even ferocity required to do the work we do.

LGBTQ People in Schools

The importance of the work the Pink TIGers strive to do in the state of Ohio is evident in the preceding description, but we also know this work to be imperative in schools across the United States. According to GLSEN's 2007 school climate survey:

- 86.2% of LGBT students experienced harassment at school in the past year
- 60.8% felt unsafe at school because of sexual orientation
- 32.7% skipped a day of school in the past month because of feeling unsafe

Such a negative educational environment hinders these students' grades and graduation rates (Kosckiw et al., 2008). When teachers work against heterosexism and homophobia in a school, by penalizing and preventing homophobic comments and actions, for example, things are better for the students in that school. Unfortunately, though, "less than a fifth of the students reported that school personnel frequently intervened ('most of the time' or 'always') when homophobic remarks and negative remarks about gender expression were made in their presence (17.6% and 14.6%, respectively)" (p. 20). Moreover, "nearly two-thirds of students reported hearing school staff make homophobic remarks" (p. 21). And even though "eight out of ten students could identify at least one school staff member whom they believed was supportive of LGBT students at their school" (p. 100), "only a tenth (10.5%) of all students in the survey were exposed to positive representations of LGBT people, history, or events in their classes" (p. 99). Clearly, teachers need opportunities to educate themselves and one another about how to work against heterosexism and homophobia and for the rights of LGBT people in their unique classrooms and schools. The teacher inquiry group described here represents one such opportunity.

Teacher Inquiry and Community Activism

Teacher research is the systematic and intentional inquiry of a teacher into his or her own practice (Cochran-Smith & Lytle, 1993). Teacher research makes important contributions to teacher education and educational research by providing insights that can be gleaned only by someone who spends extensive periods of time with students in schools doing the arduous and important work of teaching and navigating parental, administrative, and even federal expectations. It entails the documentation of, examination of, and reflection on one's practice for the purpose of gaining insights that serve to strengthen that practice and often to share those insights with others so that they too might reflect on their practice in an more informed way.

The work of the Pink TIGers is located quite particularly within the larger body of scholarship of teacher inquiry or research. That is, the group aligns itself with teacher research focused on literacy, broadly speaking, because so many Pink TIGers are English language arts teachers and because our National Council of Teachers of English (NCTE)–funded project centered on the use of literature and film. More important, our group aligns itself with research conducted in teacher communities, as opposed to teacher researchers who work independently from one another (Allen, 1999; Cochran-Smith & Lytle, 1993). Finally, and perhaps most important, we aligned ourselves with teacher inquiry conducted in the name of social change (Ballenger, 1998; Fecho, 2003; Gallas, 1997; Hankins, 2003; Hermann-Wilmarth, 2005; Trotman, 1997). Because we are an inquiry *group*, and because we are committed to social change, we came to understand our teacher research as community activism.

Lorde (1984) asserts that "without community there is no liberation" (p. 112), but the inverse is not necessarily true. That is to say, liberation demands community, but community does not necessarily provoke liberation. We know, for example, that inequitable power dynamics exist in LGBTQ communities (Blackburn, 2003). According to Esterberg (1997), in her work on lesbian and bisexual identities, a community must be diverse in order to be what she calls a "strategy for social change" (p. 175). Moreover, Cohen (2005), in her work in Black queer studies, claims that communities must "be complicated and destabilized through a recognition of the multiple subject positions and relations to dominant power" (p. 44). It is this kind of community that the group strives to be, and in doing so, it must recognize that it is not a "stable, geographically bounded entity" (Esterberg, 1997, p. 11) and it does not necessarily "share a common vision and grand agenda" (p. 176). Instead, it is more like Esterberg's conception of community, that is, having multiple centers and fuzzy boundaries and being grounded in action. She argues that by "engaging in social and political actions with others [we] creat[e] new network links. . . . We stretch ourselves. In learning to work with others who are different, we learn new tools for social and political action" (p. 176). This notion of community is foundational to the work of the Pink TIGers.

We highlight these conceptions of teacher inquiry and community to clarify, for others, how we came to see ourselves as an activist, teacher-inquiry community. This wasn't a magical happening; it did not occur overnight. And naming ourselves as such—"a community of inquiry"— did not automatically make it so. Being an activist, teacher-inquiry community is an ongoing, thought-filled process. Writing this book has allowed—indeed, required—us to be even more reflective and explicit about that process. It has forced us to look at the theories that inform our understandings of research (Allen, 1999; Cochran-Smith & Lytle, 1993) and community (Esterberg, 1997) and to put these understandings into contact with other theories that inform our thinking about sexuality, gender identity, and race (Cohen, 2005; Finnerty, 2004). Our passions for social justice fueled us to pursue equity for LGBTQ people and fight against heterosexism and homophobia in our classrooms, schools, and neighborhoods. For those readers interested in forming similar groups, we would urge you to start there. Name your passions and find others who share them. Consider teacher inquiry as one approach to the research that will inform your activism—a systematic way to learn from your teaching, your students, and one another. You may become a community, albeit yours will likely be different from ours, depending on who constitutes your group; the differences that you bring; and ultimately, the theories that inform your understandings of when, where, why, and how a community *is*. For now, we invite you to join our group and to read what we did, how we did it and why, and what we learned as members of the Pink TIGers.

Pink TIGers

Our group has met continually since the summer of 2004. Across that time, 18 people have come to at least one group meeting, and eight have participated across all 4 years. The four of us (Mollie, Caroline, Lauren, and Jill) are among those seven, along with contributors Jeane and Anette Melvin. Jim Buckley, one of our cofounding members, participated for the 1st and 2nd year but discontinued for health reasons and has since passed away. Another teacher came for the 2nd and 3rd years. Four others came the 3rd and 4th years. One teacher came for just our 2nd year. The remaining 4 teachers of the 18 came just one or two times. Additionally, there is a broader network of people we have come to know in sharing our work in our teaching and at conferences; Lesley, for example. These people are interested in what we are doing and want to be a part of it, even though they do not live in central Ohio. (Lesley has moved to Pennsylvania since

2004). They are a significant part of our group through our email Listserv. No pseudonyms are used for group members in this book.

The 14 people who attended for extended periods of time are the general focus of this book, with specific attention paid to the 11 who have written chapters in it. That is, we talk here about the 14 regular participants because all of us played significant roles in our teacher inquiry group, but we talk more about the chapter authors because you, as readers, will get to know them best in reading their chapters. Among the 14, there are elementary, secondary, and university teachers, although the majority of us are secondary English teachers. We live, teach, and meet in central Ohio, in rural, suburban, and urban contexts, and have diverse teaching experiences. Our diversity in terms of gender, race, and class is more limited. We are predominantly female; there are three males in the group, and none of us self-identifies as transgender. Only one of us self-identifies as a person of color. And while we come from diverse class backgrounds, we are currently a predominantly middle-class group of educators. There are three lesbians and one gay man among us; the rest of us are allies. Our diversity, albeit limited, is what we have come to understand as both a source of struggle and strength.

There is, however, so much more to us than our demographic data reveals (see Table 1.1). We are the Pink TIGers, and each of us brought to and sought from the group different things. Were you to come to a Saturday morning meeting, you would find something like this. We meet at Jill's gorgeous house, enjoying moist, freshly baked coffee cake; fresh fruit; and a butternut squash frittata. Jill hosts us often, and always, the food is phenomenal. We've been meeting for years and know one another fairly well. We sprawl out across chairs and the couch and the floor in a jagged shape that wants to be a circle.

Jill, straight ally, high school teacher, and doctoral candidate, is fierce and feisty. She joined the group looking for support as she advised a gay-straight alliance (GSA) under an extremely homophobic administrator and brought her thorough approach to combating this homophobia all the way to the district level to make her school safe for LGBTQ students.

Next, Anette, an out lesbian, brought both provocative questions and an openness to whatever answers came. A doctoral candidate and former elementary school teacher, she wondered what place her identity as a lesbian had in school, what relevance her sexuality had in a classroom, how that intersected with her biracial identity and race more broadly. When we meet at her house, she always has good coffee and lots of it.

TABLE 1.1. Demographics of Pink TIGers

	Teaching				Identity			Pink TIGers	
	Grade level	Content Area	Context	Start of Career	Gender	Race/Ethnicity	Lesbian, Gay, or Ally	Years of participation	Chapter in This Book
Anette	University/Elementary	Early Childhood Education	Urban	1991	Woman	Biracial	Lesbian	Years 1–4	9
Ariel	Secondary	English	Suburban	2007	Woman	White	Ally	Year 4	6
Caroline	University	English Education	Urban	1986	Woman	White	Ally	Years 1–4	1 & 3
Dana	Secondary	English	Urban	2001	Woman	White	Ally	Years 1–4	6
Deborah	Secondary	English	Suburban	1995	Woman	White	Ally	Year 2	–
Jason	Secondary	English	Urban	2005	Man	White	Ally	Years 2–3	5
Jeane	University	Literacy & Multicultural Education	Rural & Urban	1993	Woman	White	Ally	Years 1–4	2
Jill	Secondary	English	Suburban	1996	Woman	White	Ally	Years 1–4	1 & 11
Jim	University	English	Rural	1993	Man	White	Gay	Years 1–2	–
Kathy	Secondary	Counselor	Suburban		Woman	White	Ally	Year 4	–
Lauren	Secondary	English	Urban	2002	Woman	White	Lesbian	Years 1–4	1, 4, & 11
Mindy	Elementary/K–12 Professional Development	Language Arts/Multicultural Education	Suburban	1987	Woman	White	Ally	Years 2–4	7
Mollie	University	Literacy Education	Urban	1991	Woman	White	Lesbian	Years 1–4	1, 10, & 11
Ryan	Secondary	English	Suburban	2007	Man	White	Ally	Year 4	6

As an out lesbian high school teacher, Lauren came to the group with her (at the time) unique perspective as an out teacher, hesitant to incorporate queer-inclusive texts into her curriculum, fearful that parents would accuse her of trying to make their children gay. The accusations did happen, eventually, and strangely, fortunately, she lived through and beyond it.

There's Jeane. A straight ally who was one of the founders of the group, Jeane brought experience as a teacher educator in a rural campus, working to prepare her students to advocate for social justice for all students, but particularly for LGBTQ students, in their schools.

Jim, Jeane's rural campus colleague, the only man in our group initially, and one of the founders of the TIGers, brought us much humor and an inexhaustible well of knowledge, especially about 19th-century American literature. As an out gay English professor, he strove to make students aware of the various sexualities of the authors they read in his class. He came to the group looking for ways to further queer his curriculum in his American literature survey course and his 19th-century American literature course.

Ryan Schey and Ariel Uppstrom, allies, brought their passion and energy to the group. They came as 1st-year teachers who'd got jobs in the same large, rural town high school and had dived in to advise a GSA as they started their careers. They came to the TIGers seeking advice on navigating subtle and not so subtle school politics and to share their many successes.

Deborah, a straight ally and high school teacher, took over Jill's GSA when Jill left for a sabbatical. She came to the TIGers looking for support and guidance and to share the many ideas and resources that had worked for her in advising the GSA.

Jason Gonzales, a straight ally, joined us in our 2nd year as a new advisor of an extant GSA in his 1st full year of teaching at an urban arts high school known for its gay friendliness. He brought to the group a theoretical framework for doing activist work with students and was looking for practical solutions to issues he ran into.

Kristen, a straight ally and a guidance counselor who'd been approached by students to start a GSA in her high school, came to the group with her enthusiasm and openness to learn what she needed to know to start a GSA.

Mollie, a frequent hoster, a teacher educator and out lesbian, and one of the founders of the TIGers, brought a wealth of experience teaching, volunteering, and doing qualitative research with queer youth. She came in search of community to support her efforts in promoting social justice in schools.

Mindy Hall is a straight ally, elementary school teacher, and district international and multicultural coordinator. She brought to the group her passion for social justice and came to the group looking for resources she could use to educate teachers in her suburban district about the issues that affect LGBTQ people.

Dana, a straight ally, brought much hospitality and compassion to the group. She came to the group dissatisfied with an administrator who just wanted her to change the name of the GSA she was trying to help students start to the more ambiguous title "Cultural Diversity Club."

Caroline, a straight ally, a founder, and another frequent hoster, brought relentless questions, always pushing us to think further about the issues at hand and offering suggestions for people looking for suggestions. She came seeking ways to refine her curriculum to better prepare preservice teachers to address issues of homophobia and heterosexism in their schools and classrooms.

We offer you the details of the Pink TIGers in part to bring to life the people you will come to know as you read this book, but also to underscore the significance of each individual as a unique and complicated contributor to our activist community. Just as time and place matter, so do the people involved.

Finding Questions, Searching for Answers

We recognize that our inquiry cannot be done in just the same way in a different time and place by different people; and even if it could, we do not believe that the results would be predictable. We name our questions and describe our efforts at answering them, both collectively and individually, not to provide a blueprint of an inquiry but to provide an image of one way, indeed our way, of going about becoming an antihomophobia activist community.

Our inquiry was initially guided by this question:

- How can we as educators combat heterosexism and homophobia in our classrooms and schools through the use of literature and film?

However, in our 1st year, this question demanded that we consider other preliminary questions, such as:

- What do heterosexism and homophobia look like in our classrooms, schools, and lives?
- What do race and racism have to do with our commitments?
- What does religion have to do with our work?
- How do we recognize heterosexism, homophobia, and racism in ourselves and in those with whom we share our lives?
- How can we work against such forms of oppression?

To answer or at least respond to these questions, we watched and discussed films, such as *It's Elementary: Talking About Gay Issues in School* (Cohen & Chasnoff, 1996) and the "Sugartime!" (2005) episode of *Postcards from Buster*, which focused on a family with two moms. We also read and discussed literature, such as Finnerty's (2004) "An Open Letter to My White Lesbian, Gay, Bisexual, Transgender Sisters and Brothers," hooks's (2000) "Homophobia in Black Communities," and Reeves's (1999) "All God's Children." (See the Annotated Bibliography at the end of this book for a comprehensive list of the texts we shared as a teacher inquiry group.)

Moreover, our exploration has taken us beyond the confines of our Saturday morning meetings. Many of us facilitated our schools' GSAs; three of us volunteered at a youth center for lesbian, gay, bisexual, transgender, and questioning (LGBTQ) youth; most of us participated in a local rally against Issue 1; several of us engaged in media activism by writing letters in support of the "Sugar Time" episode of *Postcards from Buster*; several of us marched in the local Gay Pride parade; and several of us and our students spoke at the statehouse encouraging legislators to include enumerated language, such as that concerning LGBT people, in their antibullying policy. As a group, we attended films, lectures, and readings. More recently, we hosted a screening of *It's Elementary* (Cohen & Chasnoff, 1996) and *It's Still Elementary* (Chasnoff & Chen, 2007). Following the films, several of us served on a panel to discuss how this work takes shape in our local schools. After that, we gave currently practicing teachers the related curriculum guide (Chung & Courville, 2008) and their choice of three books: *Asha's Mums* (Elwin & Paulse, 1990), from the film; *And Tango Makes Three* (Richardson & Parnell, 2005), from the curriculum guide; and *Am I Blue? Coming Out from the Silence* (Bauer, 1994), a collection of short stories more appropriate for middle and high school students.

In addition to carrying out our activist efforts in and beyond our regular meetings, we strove to answer our questions by documenting and analyzing our interactions at monthly meetings. Each meeting of the group was audiotaped, and every audiotape was transcribed. The transcripts were then reviewed, edited, and revised by a member of the group. Also, notes were taken at each meeting. These notes were taken by one member, reviewed first by another member, and then sent to the group with an invitation to edit and revise them. Documents were collected from the meetings, particularly texts that we read and discussed together. These data, combined with interviews Mollie conducted with various group members, informed Chapters 1, 10, and 11 of this book.

This collective work was complemented by group participants conducting individual projects. All participants in these projects are named by pseudonyms and all schools and districts are unnamed. These projects provide the content for Chapters 2 through 9. Jeane Copenhaver-Johnson has written Chapter 2, which captures her struggle as a teacher educator with a resistant student. Thus, it demonstrates the importance and challenge of antihomophobia work in teacher preparation. Chapter 3, by Caroline Clark, takes a broader look, examining Caroline's teaching over time, thus revealing the complexity of what it means to do antihomophobia, antiheterosexism work in classrooms—her own and her students'. The following five chapters provide practical models from teachers doing this work in K–12 classrooms, schools, and districts. Chapter 4, by Lauren Kenney, offers the perspective of a gay teacher coming out, being out, and working against homophobia and heterosexism and ultimately transphobia in her classroom and school. Jason Gonzales, who wrote Chapter 5, describes a new teacher's burgeoning efforts to engage LGBTQ topics through critical inquiry in both his classroom and GSA. Chapter 6 is coauthored by Ryan Schey and Ariel Uppstrom. Together, they describe their experience of taking over the GSA at their high school during their 1st year of teaching. Chapter 7 is an account by Mindy Hall, an elementary school teacher and multicultural coordinator, working against homophobia in her various professional positions. Jill Smith wrote Chapter 8 to tell the story of her development as a straight ally and the resistances and responses she experienced in her classroom, school, and district. Chapter 9, by Anette Melvin, questions assumptions about the intersections of race and sexuality though an analysis of interviews with one White and two African American lesbian teachers who are closeted in their schools. And Chapter 10, by Mollie Blackburn, examines how our diversity, though limited, and our work across lines of difference contributed to our becoming an activist community. Not one of these chapters provides answers to the specific questions we have raised, but together they create a sort of response to them. In Chapter 11, we synthesize this collective response and discuss our work as a potential catalyst for further movement and positive change. We hope the collective inquiry and activism of the Pink TIGers will provoke you, wherever you are, enough to join us in combating homophobia and heterosexism in classrooms and schools, in whatever way you can. Now.

Note

1. You will notice that sometimes we use the acronym LGBT and other times LGBTQ. When we are pointing to a source, we use what the source uses; sources may include scholarship, newspaper articles, students, and so on. Otherwise, we are deliberate in our choices, using *lesbian and gay* when we realize we are failing to include bisexual and transgender people, adding the *Q* when we want to include people questioning their sexual identities, and using *queer* when referencing people who are not heteronormative without imposing classifications among those people. We strive to be as inclusive and specific as possible, always prioritizing inclusivity.

References

Allen, J. E. (Ed.). (1999). *Class actions: Teaching for social justice in elementary and middle school*. New York: Teachers College Press.

Ballenger, C. (1998). *Teaching other people's children: Literacy and learning in a bilingual classroom*. New York: Teachers College Press.

Bauer, M. D. (1994). *Am I blue? Coming out from the silence*. New York: Harper-Collins.

Blackburn, M. V. (2003). Exploring literacy performances and power dynamics at the Loft: Queer youth reading the world and word. *Research in the Teaching of English, 37*(4), 467–490.

Blackburn, M. V., & Buckley, J. F. (2005). Teaching queer-inclusive English language arts. *Journal of Adolescent and Adult Literacy, 49*(3), 202–212.

Chasnoff, D. (Producer/Director), & Chen, S. (Producer). (2007). *It's still elementary* [Motion picture]. (Available from Groundspark, San Francisco, CA.)

Chung, C., & Courville, M. (2008). *It's elementary: A guide to community organizing, professional development, and K–8 curriculum*. San Francisco: The Respect for All Project, a Program of Groundspark.

Cochran-Smith, M., & Lytle, S. (1993). *Inside/outside: Teacher research and knowledge*. New York: Teachers College Press.

Cohen, C. J. (2005). Punks, bulldaggers, and welfare queens: The radical potential of queer politics. In E. P Johnson & M. G. Henderson (Eds.), *Black queer studies: A critical anthology* (pp. 21–51). Durham, NC: Duke University Press.

Cohen, H. S. (Producer), & Chasnoff, D. (Producer/Director). (1996). *It's elementary: Talking about gay issues in school* [Motion picture]. (Available from Women's Educational Media, San Francisco, CA.)

Elwin, R., & Paulse, M. (1990). *Asha's mums.* London: Women's Press.

Esterberg, K. G. (1997). *Lesbian and bisexual identities: Constructing communities, constructing selves.* Philadelphia: Temple University Press.

Fecho, B. (2003). *"Is this English?": Race, language, and culture in the classroom.* New York: Teachers College Press.

Finnerty, D. (2004). *An open letter to my White lesbian, gay, bisexual, transgender sisters and brothers.* Retrieved June 8, 2009, from http://www.tolerance.org/images/teach/current/Open_Letter.pdf

Gallas, K. (1997). *Sometimes I can be anything: Power, gender, and identity in a primary classroom.* New York: Teachers College Press.

GLSEN's Ally Week FAQs. (2008). Retrieved May 4, 2009, from http://www.allyweek.org/about/index.cfm

Gunther, J. (Director). (2005, March 22). *Postcards from Buster:* "Sugartime!" [Television broadcast]. Columbus, OH: Public Broadcasting Service.

Hankins, K. (2003). *Teaching through the storm: A journal of hope.* New York: Teachers College Press.

Hermann-Wilmarth, J. M. (2005). *Co-constructions of meaning through dialogue: The intersections of homosexuality and religion in a preservice teacher/instructor inquiry group.* Unpublished dissertation, University of Georgia.

hooks, b. (2000). Homophobia in black communities. In D. Constantine-Simms (Ed.), *The greatest taboo: Homosexuality in Black communities* (pp. 67–73). Los Angeles: Alyson Books.

Kosciw, J. G., Diaz, E. M., & Greytak, E. A. (2008). *The 2007 National School Climate Survey: The experiences of lesbian, gay, bisexual, and transgender youth in our nation's schools.* New York: GLSEN.

Lorde, A. (1984). *Sister outsider.* Berkeley, CA: The Crossing Press.

Reeves, K. E. (1999). All God's children. *Essence, 30*(7), 220.

Richardson, J., & Parnell, P. (2005). *And Tango makes three.* New York: Simon & Schuster.

Trotman, M. V. (1997). "Would Queenie be in our class?": Critiquing social inequity in schools. *The New Advocate, 11*(1), 55–65.

2

Learning About Heterosexism as a Teacher Educator

The Resistant Student as Catalyst for Change

JEANE F. COPENHAVER-JOHNSON

FOR NEARLY 13 YEARS, I have challenged homophobia and heterosexism in university coursework I teach and have encouraged students to critically analyze systems of privilege that undermine fair, equitable societies. In our teacher education program, I teach, among others, a course that feels to me like the Single Course in Multicultural Education (SCME) (Marshall, 1999; Sleeter, 2001). While it is not the only course in our program in which issues of multicultural education are addressed, it is the only course in which the focus is entirely on culturally relevant and social justice–oriented teaching, and depending on the particular mix of courses my students take, some report it as the only course in which issues of sexuality are discussed.

The preservice and practicing teachers enrolled in this course arrive with a range of lifelong beliefs about privilege and equity, and they—of course—sometimes resist my perspectives and assert their own Truths. I expect this to occur (Damico & Quay, 2006; Eyre, 1993; McIntyre, 2002; Solomon, Portelli, Daniel, & Campbell, 2005; Wood, 2005). Given what we know about racial identity development, for example, I believe that such resistance may be the first step toward deconstructing long-held understandings (Tatum, 1992) and be critical to the dialogue that prompts our growth across various areas of social justice concerns.

For these reasons, I attempt to challenge, rather than alienate, students as we engage in critical discussions about systems that enable race, ability, gender, linguistic, class, and heterosexual privilege. I invite students to tell their stories about such issues, for personal narratives have compelling power in helping students rethink issues of privilege and oppression (Davis, 1992, Goodman, 2000; Stoddart, 1991; Vicars, 2006). To facilitate our discussions, I assign readings that counter stereotypes with accurate information and with emotion, ask questions that will help us analyze our own positions and responsibilities, and tell stories of my own development as someone committed to social justice. Dialogue cannot occur if students are imposed upon and begin to simply teacher-please. Therefore, I have purposefully made spaces within the course for students to express, and analyze, the ways our course content connects to, conflicts with, and extends their own experiences and beliefs.

In this chapter, I share the story of my experience with a resistant student, the teaching insights this experience has posed for me, and the changes in my practice that have resulted from my reflection on the experience. Since the student has no opportunity to assert the Truths of his experience, I use a pseudonym (Kyle) and change identifying details about our interactions. Like Cochran-Smith (2000), I tell a fiction that is my best recollection of the events and my interpretations of them. The student's recollections would likely be different from mine, and the classmates' recollections would likely be different from ours (see, e.g., Fishman & McCarthy, 2005). I will, however, talk about *my* experiences and learning related to Kyle's participation—resistance to participation, really—in my course. This remains a painful story, for it has revealed to me assumptions I have made about my own practice of engaged pedagogy. As hooks (1994) explains:

> Engaged pedagogy does not seek simply to empower students. Any classroom that employs a holistic model of learning will also be a place where teachers grow, and are empowered by the process. That empowerment cannot happen if we refuse to be vulnerable while encouraging students to take risks. Professors who expect students to share confessional narratives but who are themselves unwilling to share are exercising power in a manner that could be coercive. In my classrooms, I do not expect students to take any risks that I would not take, to share in any way that I would not share. (p. 21)

In telling this story about my own learning as a social justice teacher-educator, I follow my commitment to engaging in learning alongside my students. This story follows a narrative inquiry tradition (Clandinin & Connelly, 2000) and a tradition of university teacher–researchers (e.g.,

Cochran-Smith, 2000; Fishman & McCarthy, 2005; Leland & Harste, 2005; Milner, 2007; Willis, 2003) engaged in self-study in order to better match social justice goals to the teaching/learning actions that promote social justice. To reconstruct and analyze this story, I have consulted textual resources developed at the time that some of these events occurred—resources such as email messages to a colleague, the course syllabus, my writing to the resistant student, my in-class inquiry project write-ups, conversation transcripts—and a journal I began keeping once I initiated my formal reflective inquiry about this experience. Despite my attempts to use these documents to "freeze specific moments in the narrative inquiry space" (Clandinin & Connelly, 2000, p. 83), these reflections may or may not reflect the perspectives of others who shared the following experiences with me. These reflections represent my efforts to better understand my experiences.

Designing a Social Justice Course

I designed this graduate multicultural education course, one I teach regularly, around several focus areas. Our 10-week quarter gives us enough time to only briefly survey issues, and I acknowledge, but cannot change, this limitation. The class enrollment ranges from a low of approximately 10 students to as high as the mid-20s, and students and I generally meet once a week for 2½ hours. Given the scant evidence that traditional multicultural education courses (or in-service programming) result in long-term shifts in graduates' attitudes and behaviors (Sleeter, 2001), I designed this course to be inquiry-oriented in nature—a place to accumulate accurate information, to have new experiences, and to instill curiosity.

The scholarship we review moves from a focus on issues of race, to issues of class, to issues of gender, and so forth until we reach a time in the quarter when I believe that we are ready to more explicitly focus on issues of homophobia and heteronormativity. I do not postpone these deeper conversations until later in the quarter because I believe they are "delicate" or problematic. I postpone them because they are, for my mostly White, mostly straight-identified, mostly middle-class teacher-students, the conversations they are most inexperienced having in a public space with an authority figure, and regardless of my desire to share power with my students, the reality of the imbalance in our power puts me at risk of indoctrination (Freedman, 2007). Although students report that they sometimes self-edit when we converse about race, they nearly always indicate their hesitancy when we discuss sexuality—evidenced by statements such as "I'm not sure I'm going to say this right, but . . ." or "Please don't think I'm a bigot when you hear this but . . ." or even by remaining silent until *after* class to speak to me individually about their questions, concerns, and insights about the topic (similar to Winans, 2006).

Like Athaneses and Larrabee (2003), I recognize the potential risk of "essentializing" (p. 242) the stories of GLBT people by separating out groups commonly identified as "other" during this course. However, I also recognize that many of my students have been deprived of accurate information about the histories of GLBT people, the forms of oppression GLBT people continue to face, and the narratives of experience some GLBT people have been willing to share. Most of my students identify (or accept a social identification by others) as heterosexual, and heteronormativity has enabled them to remain comfortably ignorant of heterosexism— at least consciously. My students also tend to overwhelmingly identify as Christian, an identification that occasionally leads to dissonance in their considerations of heterosexism and homophobia (see Athanases & Larrabee, 2003; Deeb-Sossa & Kane, 2007; Griffin & Ouellett, 2003; Maney & Cain, 1997; Robinson & Ferfolja, 2001; Winans, 2006). In the time we have, we are limited to developing an acquaintance with the content, fostering curiosity, nurturing a sense of responsibility to know/learn more, and teaching strategies for social action.

I try to engage students in less rather than more threatening ways. While threat is unavoidable and necessary in critical inquiry settings (Fecho, 2000), I know no balance that will allow me to feel that I have completely honored my stances *and* my students' stances concurrently. I am not saying I perceive or validate every point of view as equally relevant or acceptable, but I cannot move my students toward new understandings if I fail to respectfully recognize and try to understand the stances that inform their current beliefs (Chizhik & Chizhik, 2005). McLaren (2003) explains:

> The critical educator doesn't believe that there are two sides to every question, with both sides needing equal attention. For the critical educator, there are *many* sides to a problem, and often these sides are linked to certain class, race, and gender interests. (p. 71, emphasis in original)

One of the assignments I have developed for this particular class, to begin exploring how the "sides of a problem" we see are connected to our experiences, is a response journal. In this journal, I attempt to make a place for students to express, in writing, the memories, reflections, confusions, and other connections that are posed for them in class. It is designed to be a space for students to reflect privately (albeit with me). The guidelines for this assignment are noted in the syllabus as follows:

> You will maintain a *weekly* journal in which you respond to the readings and class discussions. This should be a place for thoughtful issue raising and serious searches for tentative answers to dilemmas. I encourage you to share these journal entries with one another if you feel comfortable doing so. The journal may also be used to question class discussions, ask questions directly of me, and generally do some mental/emotional "work" with the content of the class. The journal will be submitted twice. [Dates and procedures are described here]. Journals may be handwritten or typewritten.

Students first submit their work to me midterm (5th week), an arrangement I developed when it seemed that responding to individual entries felt too segmented, since the larger issues behind students' responses usually became evident only after multiple entries. This schedule was also devised to permit students to submit their first private work after having some time to get to know, and develop trust with, me. Willis (2003) describes students' use of "public voices" early in the term, indicating of students' early writings that

> students tend to respond in ways they believe are non-offensive or tolerant early in the semester. Generally, as their understandings about the classroom climate, interpretive community, and basic student-to-student and student-to-instructor trust grows so does their ability to share more comfortably and confidently. (p. 55)

I have purposefully constructed this assignment—and *only* this assignment—"loosely" in an effort to create these spaces for students to express, and then challenge, their own thinking outside the class discussions. It allows me, in my responses to them, to participate in that process, too—asking questions, telling my own stories, and learning what's on their minds so I can bring in responsive resources. Others have suggested the importance of professors sharing their own narratives (e.g., Davis, 1992;

Milner, 2007). For some students, the journal dialogue functions as a sort of rehearsal for what will occur in class. Overall, it reassures them that they don't have to think, believe, or value exactly as I do to have a strong academic, and even life-changing, experience in the course. This is not the only course assignment students complete, but it is the assignment most important to the narrative I share here.

My Encounter with the Resistant Student

Some time ago, I taught this multicultural education course to a group of approximately 15 classroom teachers. I felt excited about the class and comfortable with the group, except for one student who remained silent all term. Initially, I that thought Kyle was, perhaps, shy or even depressed; in the past, I have encountered a number of such students. However, in the first journal submission, Kyle responded to readings about economic disparities (e.g., Shipler, 2004) by dismissing the initiative of the poor. After reading McIntosh (1989) and Shipler (1997), which focus on issues of race and White privilege, Kyle denied the existence of racism and claimed that the readings I assigned were not scholarly. The student explained away every example of social inequities, in our readings or discussions, as isolated instances *or* as the result of people failing to work hard— blaming "lazy" parents and expressing that what researchers had perceived as racist acts or institutionalized racism were, in fact, not so. Reading the response journal made my eyes burn. My stomach became upset, and I could hear my heart pound. I have encountered skeptical, or even angry, students many times, but this journal struck me as particularly caustic. Something about Kyle's words differed from those of other students I had met, and with whom I had learned, in the past 13 years. I also realized that the student's in-class silence had been a form of resistance (see, e.g., Ladson-Billings, 1996), not deference.

I responded to this first journal submission by writing back to Kyle, as I did each student. It took a long time to muster the courage to compose my responses. As I prepared to write this chapter about my experience, I recalled myself as having been angry and directive in my writing. However, I felt surprise as I reread my comments and questions, once some time had passed, and noted how desperately I had tried to find points of agreement with the student so that my questioning would not convey an alienating tone. Regardless of how angry the journal responses had made me, I wanted to respect the spirit of trust in which the journal assignment itself was designed. Therefore, in my responses, I struggled, as Wood (2005) has explained, "to keep my subjectivity at bay" (p. 436). I questioned to learn more about how Kyle was interpreting the text and remarked how reader-response theory might help us understand how our readings (mine and Kyle's) were so discrepant. The student had worked with people of poverty in former employment, and I asked how these prior experiences might have influenced reactions to the text *The Working Poor: Invisible in America* (Shipler, 2004). When Kyle told the story of family economic hardships, and parents' sacrifices to ensure Kyle's education (and then condemned families who expected handouts rather than working for economic autonomy), I shared my own experience of growing up in a working-class home and observed how those of us who have been able to escape poverty sometimes expect that others can do so also.

And on and on it went, for nearly five single-spaced pages, these responses to Kyle's journal and my invitations for us to learn together about how our lives had influenced our experiences with the scholarship. I made a deliberate effort to stifle my feelings of defensiveness and to quiet the anger I felt at the characterizations of economically poor individuals as "lazy" or perhaps not well suited for a college-preparatory K–12 experience. I truly did want to know *why* Kyle perceived the world this way and what the source of this anger had been. I wondered if Kyle was trying to avoid having to admit that privilege resulted less from meritocracy than from systems of inequality in society. I expected my responses, despite the care with which they were drafted, would be angering.

After the next class session, however, I handed back the journals, and Kyle disappeared. The dreaded conversation/confrontation did not occur. No emails were exchanged, and Kyle never stopped in for office hours.

Brief discussions about homophobia and heterosexism occurred in each class meeting, even when not prompted by the assigned readings, but we later spent a week focused specifically on antihomophobic teaching and in discussions of the realities that gay, lesbian, bisexual, and transgender students face in schools by reviewing work like the GLSEN surveys (Kosciw, 2004) and videos like *It's Elementary* (Cohen & Chasnoff, 1997). We read a hopeful selection of fiction, including the short story "Am I Blue?" (Coville, 1994), as well as narratives of strong young people such as those published in the "Youth Voices" article in the LGBT special issue of the *Harvard Educational Review*. During the class in which our discussions focused on teaching against homophobia and heterosexism, Kyle would not look up, participate in small-group talk, or watch the video. When I discussed legislation about gay and lesbian adoptive families, Kyle moved uncomfortably, writing in a notebook, and then left the moment class was over—having interacted with no one.

In retrospect, and I will explore this feeling more fully later, I notice how desperately I hoped Kyle *would* remain silent. I was afraid that this student's comments would threaten other students and the sense of community the others of us had developed, undermine the authority of the texts we shared in class, and provoke a confrontation I wasn't prepared to handle. Kyle cooperated with my unspoken/unconscious wishes, came in quietly, left promptly, and never responded to me about my responses to the journal.

Our eventual confrontation followed Kyle's submission of a blank page in the next response journal. Invoking religious objections to our readings about GLBTQ issues, Kyle refused to do any of the readings. At this point, I asked for a meeting; I was unable to grade the journal without responses to the readings. When we met to discuss this choice not to complete the assignment, Kyle's fear of the texts became apparent; Kyle felt unable to even *look* at the readings because to do so would be to compromise an unquestioned religious faith—as if one could be soiled or damned just *by reading* the texts. Kyle stated that there was *no* relationship between issues of homophobia and elementary classroom teaching. None. Homosexuality is a sin, period. It's wrong. Research that indicates otherwise is not research. Teaching children that it is okay is wrong.

For a moment, my feelings of anger began to change to compassion and pity. Suddenly, I understood that this student was *afraid* of our texts, and Kyle was *afraid* of any learning that might challenge his ability to uncritically accept what authority figures in life had been teaching for years. While Kyle argued against texts focused on racism, class issues, gender bias, and others, Kyle found it completely unacceptable to explore any issues facing GLBTQ people because, simply, the faith-based explanations (e.g., being a person who identifies as nonheterosexual is being a person engaged, willfully, in sin) were irreconcilable with our class discussions, and, in fact, the ideas I was teaching were dangerous.

Trying to understand these perspectives better, I examined materials by a faith-based authority whom many of my Christian students admire, Dr. James Dobson. As a subset of Dobson's Focus on the Family ministries, "Focus on Your Child" (Focus on the Family, 2007) notes, "Amidst the barrage of questions [about homosexuality], we must first turn to God's

Word—our ultimate authority—for answers." Further on this same page, Dobson himself notes that "opposition to the gay and lesbian tidal wave is not an expression of hate but one of *social justice*" (emphasis mine). His group believes that Christians are marginalized, that there is "no evidence" that homosexuals are "disadvantaged," and that young people are put in danger by educational programs that infiltrate schools in the form of "tolerance training" and gay-straight alliances that [purportedly] encourage youth to experiment with homosexuality (see also "Gay Activism in Public Schools" interview link to Focus on Your Child website).

I cannot detail how this situation was resolved without revealing identifying information about the class and the student. However, I can explain that I was unhappy with the outcome. Kyle completed an alternate, but related, assignment, and I advised Kyle that our program (and, likely, any other graduate program) would require reading, analyzing, and critically evaluating scholarly materials; I recommended withdrawing from our program. Kyle submitted the work and, as usual, disappeared—from the campus but not from my thoughts.

For a time, I stewed in some anger about the episode. To me, this student exploited an assignment of my own creation, and I had, in effect, made this possible. If I had graded the blank page as just a zero, and not forced further interaction/engagement (not to suggest that I was successful in achieving engagement, but I refused to issue any grade at all with the blank page), Kyle could have still passed my class given the way I had weighted and described the course requirements. A failing grade for the course could have been successfully challenged. I was disappointed in myself that I had inadvertently created a grade structure in which Kyle's choice to refuse, because of explicit and uncensored homophobia, would not result in automatic failure. I resented having my professionalism, competence, and moral judgment questioned by this student and wondered what my legal rights were as a university faculty member—something I had never worried about before. I felt that Kyle was powerful, and I felt powerless.

As I reflected on our interactions, however, I noted that, although passionate about these convictions, Kyle probably was lashing out at the experience of relative powerlessness, too—powerlessness by being in a world (our classroom) where others' perspectives challenged the most fundamental realities of the world Kyle knew. Although I perceived no way to be successful, I carried guilt about my feeling that I had failed with Kyle—and had therefore failed the children who would be in Kyle's care.

Now that I have explored the kinds of faith-based materials that were likely part of Kyle's upbringing and belief system, and see the urgency (and understand, to some extent at least, the *certainty*) of Kyle's worries about the class's take on heterosexism and homophobia, it is clear to me that I probably would never be able to reach this student.

Time to Reflect—Alone and with TIGers

I dealt with this dilemma largely alone. I had discussed the religious objection with my administrators, my partner, and—only on a need-to-know basis—two colleagues involved in my program without identifying the student in these discussions. At a later meeting of my Pink TIGer collaborators, I decided to share this tale as an example of frustration at how my practice had failed to reach a student. I told my friends and colleagues an abbreviated version of the story (again, without identifying details) and sought their input. In retrospect, I think I craved some affirmation of my efforts, some reassurance that the blame for the situation rested with *the student* and not with *me*. As I told the story, however, two of my colleagues became increasingly angry, and they expressed that they felt the student had won—and that I had let homophobia win by permitting an alternate assignment, therefore reifying the religious objections. Other colleagues offered quiet words of support for me and outrage at the student, but my most vivid recollection of this meeting was of my surprise at my angry colleagues' reactions and my shame at taking action that was, to them, *counter* to my goals of combating homophobia and heterosexism. One colleague thought I should have done more than counsel the student out of the program; I should have ensured that my student would be removed from the program, something I did not believe could occur unless the student was failing coursework.

This was the first time in my career that I ever had experienced disapproval of my teaching or a questioning of my commitment to social justice. Until then, I had never noted the absence of negative feedback from others; it had simply never happened—and it had never crossed my mind that it would, particularly for this class. Students evaluating my teaching of the SCME at this institution and elsewhere had spoken of it as life-changing, sometimes as critical to their educational and personal journeys. They discussed the significance of our conversations about difficult issues and the dignity afforded students as they worked through them. I had often used these evaluations (as Tatum, 1992, reports) to check whether I was meeting my own goals. The discussion with my TIGer collaborators, then, reopened the wound created at the time I dealt with the student and added to it the newfound disappointment of colleagues whose opinions I deeply valued. And because I valued their opinions, I began to rethink the situation and my responsibility for it. *Was* I as committed to social justice as I believed I was? Did I have options other than those I perceived in the moment? What had I overlooked, and how could I prevent letting "homophobia win" again?

Teaching for Social Justice: Hard Contradictions

One of the dilemmas of this situation is that my initial, in-the-moment response was to find fault with the student, and then my next, defensive response was to minimize the harm I had imagined would come to the class as a whole, and to me, as a result of having the student present. In my reflection, I have not found specific alternatives to the solution I developed with the student, nor have I found methods to ensure that such a failure could be avoided in the future. What I have learned, however, is that encounters with resistant students can help us become better, more thoughtful teachers (Ladson-Billings, 1996). My teaching of the class that term had been deeply affected by Kyle's presence/threat, in ways that I later realized had prompted *me* to evoke privilege and power as protective devices. Reflecting on my experiences has taught me valuable lessons about how I responded, and wish *not* to respond in the future, to the threat posed by an overtly resistant student.

Permitting, and Even Enabling, Silence

Although committed to the belief that students must share their stories, I had not considered the significance of the stories that told Truths so different from my own that I could not treat them as parallel, experiential, social realities. When I asked Kyle why I had not been approached about his feelings about racism, classism, and homophobia much earlier in the term, Kyle replied that I would have been unable to be unbiased in my grading of the coursework—or the in-class participation. I would not have responded fairly. I reassured Kyle that I had many times taught students whose social justice commitments were very different from my own and that students could do well in the course even if they did not share my commitments. However, looking back, I know that Kyle was right. No matter how I tried, there is no way I could have integrated these perspectives (that I perceived as willfully ignorant of evidence) as valid points of view, equally worthy of consideration in classroom conversations. I think I had been, by ignoring Kyle's silences or by only conversing directly in the journal responses or in the smaller discussion groups, trying to keep Kyle from voicing these beliefs in the larger group discussion. I perceived Kyle as volatile and potentially disruptive to the "healthy" class that was, in my perception, otherwise taking place. In retrospect, this (lack of) action reflects my lack of faith in the analytical thinking I was observing among the other students in the class; my belief that Kyle's expressions would disrupt, rather than strengthen, their examinations of privilege shows how significantly I was beginning to doubt my own efficacy in the presence of such resistance.

Unlike Fishman (Fishman & McCarthy, 2005) I could not have found Kyle's perspectives on racism, classism, and homophobia to be just one more point of view, to then be questioned and interrogated. I have read of other teacher-educators who are able to invite into the conversation the stereotyped beliefs of their students and have understood the levels of complexity and challenge that have followed those conversations, including conversations where students of color or ethnic- and sexual-minority students feel further victimized. I was unwilling to allow this kind of scenario to develop in a class where many of my students were beginning to seriously reconsider their beliefs about meritocracy and about their own privilege. I worried about upsetting the progress I saw in other students. In fact, if Kyle had entered the common conversation, I would have worried that my inability to accept the Truths of Kyle's life would somehow convey to my students that I was not, after all, the trustworthy person I claimed to be. My power would be overtly expressed and available to all to see. By reinforcing Kyle's silence, however, I *was* enacting power.

It has taken some time for me to begin to rethink the situation and move the *student* from the center (as the oppressor/problem) and begin thinking about how I enabled this resistance to occur and even reinforced the skepticism about "book learning" as it contrasted with Kyle's beliefs and experiences. I had wanted to engage in a pedagogy that allowed me the sense that I was sharing power with my students, that decentered me as the conversational lead and instead focused on students' experiences and meaning-making. Other university educators have expressed that they have held a similar desire to achieve such a balance of power with students (e.g., Gardner, Dean, & McKaig, 1989; Guiterrez-Gomez, 2002; hooks, 1994) and hopefully develop "safe" spaces as a result of sharing this power. They have also shared that this process does not, in fact, necessarily result in "safe" spaces for dialogue.

My belief that my refusal of directive power was, in fact, empowering my students was not only erroneous; it also prompted me to allow the resistant student's in-class silences. Because I wished not to have to take an authority-like stand, and because of my certainty that I would need to do so if Kyle spoke, I silently wished for Kyle's involvement in the class to remain marginal. That is, if Kyle stayed silent, we would retain our "safe" community.

However, silence is problematic. Winans (2006) notes,

> I believe that instructors need to consider the nature of the silences in their classrooms—what topics and *what modes of questioning* are off-limits—and what are the consequences of this? What are the implications of avoiding issues that seem controversial or "too political," or about which we worry that students might express ignorant or hateful thoughts or feelings? (p. 105, emphasis in original)

By not allowing this challenge to the group's developing perspectives, I had deprived the students of the possibility of interrogating their own thinking—even the thinking I liked and believed evidenced growth (e.g., an early childhood teacher who admitted initially to believing that early childhood education was not affected by heterosexism but later came to identify and challenge examples of heterosexism in her child's school) and seeing how their own discussions privileged particular perspectives, histories, and values. I limited students' opportunities to defend their points of view or critique them. As Kumashiro (2004) explains, teacher educators can step back and ask, "Whom did this discussion privilege and how? What issues did this discussion ignore, and what hidden messages did those gaps convey?" (p. 114). Winans (2006) suggests asking students questions such as "Where does my knowledge come from? What is unknown to me? What is unthinkable to me and why?" (p. 105). I could have called attention to these and similar "gaps in the conversation" but did not—not with this class—although I had regularly asked similar questions with previous groups of students. Had I expressed more faith in Kyle's peers by being more directive in my participation, our conversations might have been more productive, and Kyle might have been more compelled to perceive our discussions as less "one-sided" and "biased." At the time, I thought I valued the different points of view and that they naturally emerged from the group, but I can see now that they did not—largely because of my lack of directiveness and my complicity with Kyle's silence.

Such an approach to discussion would have better prepared my students for thinking beyond the classroom and for taking difficult stands against homophobia and heterosexism outside the college classroom. I do not want students to believe that talk in class is enough to achieve a social justice disposition; action is necessary (Elhoweris, Parmeswaran, & Nemeldin, 2004). The students themselves might have been able to engage Kyle's affect (Goodman, 2000; Milner, 2007) in ways that our readings, and my commentary, could not.

Possessing No Theory of Resistance

I also noted in my reflection on this experience that I had never developed strong pedagogical perspectives regarding students who resist— who simply do not want to learn or be open to new kinds of information and perspectives. Britzman and Gilbert (2004) speak specifically about how this resistance affects teaching against homophobia and heterosexism, noting that "inquiries into understanding gayness in teacher education must take seriously the force of this passion, the fantasy that fuels the refusal, the negation, or the 'I do not want to know'" (p. 88). Indeed, every resistant student I met in the past appeared (genuinely or not, I realize) to come to a better understanding of homophobia and heterosexism by the time our SCME concluded. I note that my goals in a stand-alone course must be modest, but I have witnessed amazing changes of perspective (and the resultant discord that sometimes follows in students' relationships with others outside the class, whose Truths they then challenge) in many of my most resistant students. I have told students explicitly that we begin the course in different places, and I expect that we all grow, some more than, and some less than, others. Therefore, I had never been made to consider deeply what a failed experience might be like, how to explain it, and how to prevent it from happening. I falsely trusted myself as a teacher, the structure of our class as a place for learning, and the experiences of my former students as assurances that my course facilitated social justice dispositions and armed students with ways of thinking that would help them transform the social and educational settings in their lives. I will not make these same faulty assumptions in the future but will invest time taking on the challenge Britzman and Gilbert (2004) identify, and develop a more sound "theory of not learning" which they contend "requires an understanding of the ego defenses against or resistance to being affected by the otherness of knowledge" (p. 89). This is my personal challenge.

Guarding My Identity/Identities

A final insight I made about my practice is that, in this situation, I guarded my identity while expecting students to tell their stories and even rethink fundamental ideas about their own identities. While I believed that I participated alongside my students—completing and writing up my own inquiry projects just as they did, sharing these projects in class, telling selected stories from my life—I guarded/protected particular features of my identity, including my own heterosexuality. Like Sharkey (2004), I realize these omissions have ramifications for the authenticity of the class. Sharkey, who censored out of her writing (unintentionally) and her discussions with one of her groups of students (intentionally) her identity as a lesbian, asks, "By censoring myself, did I unintentionally censor or silence others?" (p. 507). This is a question worth exploring. When I censor my stories, will my students "read" that absence and censor their own? Greene (2003) contends, "To engage with our students as persons is to affirm our own incompleteness, our consciousness of spaces still to be explored, desires to be tapped, possibilities still to be opened and pursued" (p. 111). This distinction between what should be transparent in order to facilitate dialogue and what might be protected in self-interest is perhaps the most challenging insight I have made about my own practice and response to the resistant student.

During the term Kyle was in my class, my defensiveness led me to become more protective of my identity as the course instructor. One of the other students had commented that I seemed to let this group of students remain a bit more "comfortable" than usual, that I had handled them more delicately, and that she was surprised by this, given her prior experiences in my other classes. I had limited the experiences of other students because of my discomfort with Kyle's potential responses to those activities, readings, and discussions and my desire to retain (but not have to overtly demonstrate) power. When I noticed these absences from the class, I noted another significant change I had made to retain my power.

This term, I had not interrupted students' assumptions about my sexuality. In the dialogues I often have with students during the course, I never claim a heterosexual identity. When it comes up, I note that I am "currently identified by others as heterosexual" and that the identification yields privileges I have done nothing to earn.

Normally, I have responded to patterns that reify the naturalness of heterosexuality by engaging *queer pedagogy*. I use the term in the spirit of Sumara and Davis (1999), who explain their use of the term *"queer."*

> "Queer" is not meant as a signifier that represents gay, lesbian, bisexual, and transgendered identities. Rather, "queer" functions as a marker representing interpretive work that refuses what Halley has called "the heterosexual bribe"—that is, the cultural rewards afforded to those whose public performances of self are contained within that narrow band of behaviors considered proper to a heterosexual identity. (p. 192)

As I tiptoed though Kyle's class, I not only had restructured our in-class experiences to preserve a sense of safety (for me) in the discussions, but, in this particular class, I also did not make problematic students' assumptions about my sexuality. By choosing not to do so, I invoked heterosexual privilege to reinforce my power and credibility as the instructor of the class. To be clear, I *armed* myself with heterosexual privilege—not by taking any action but by my silence and inaction. This performative, defensive practice exploited heterosexism. My colleagues were right. At the time, I was not conscious of having made this choice—ironically, given how deliberate my other choices had been in the past—until my former student mentioned the differences between this class and others I had taught. I think this example demonstrates how pervasive heterosexism is, even for those of us who think we know better or who deliberately try to disrupt it.

Conclusions

Processing this painful story has been worthwhile and instructive for me and may have value for others engaged in teaching for social justice. Although my reflections have not resulted in the identification of specific ways to meet a resistant student's needs, they have prompted my growth as a teacher-educator trying to work against heterosexism. I am indebted to my TIGer colleagues for prompting me to consider these questions because the process has allowed me to consider ways to prevent invoking both silence and heterosexism in the future if I encounter other resistant students.

The "problem" of the resistant student does not always reside with the student. It is important to reflect on the ways in which we instructors inadvertently create environments that can reinforce resistance. While I can reconstruct my syllabus so that refusal to engage with the readings will result in a failing grade, such an effort rings of tokenism. Ensuring course failure only masks a problem—diverts it to elsewhere and ensures its indirect effects on others (namely, children). It does nothing to promote the dialogue that might foster understanding. I will need better understandings, in the future, of how the resistant, and especially homophobic, student has come to be that way, what purposes a student's silence might serve, and how to balance student engagement with a healthy understanding of the student's identity development, feelings about privilege and oppression, and history. Growing as a teacher educator means that I need to regularly interrogate the silences of my classroom, asking, as Ladson-Billings (1996) suggests, "what complicity [we, teachers] have in creating student silences" (p. 85) and also in evaluating the extent to which these silences are used as weapons to stifle dialogue.

When silence wins in a class, an opportunity to avert potential indoctrination of students by acquainting them, explicitly, with the knowledge of alternative propositions about social justice (and the critical tools to evaluate these propositions) is lost.

What is perhaps most important of all is that I have learned to attend, personally, to the potentially destructive, and defensive, performance choices teacher educators might make when faced with resistant students. The choices I made privileged heterosexism—both by my falling short of providing my students with opportunities to hold the kinds of challenging conversations needed to facilitate deep changes of perspective on social justice (and signifying, implicitly, issues of race, class, and sexuality as "controversial") and because I accepted the privileges that heterosexual identifications afford. Permitting students to define me as heterosexual (the absence of any alternative performance or disclosure constituting such an action), I was enabled to resist the kind of identity that might challenge my authority in a class where the resistant student's presence prompted me to doubt my efficacy. Talburt (2000) makes clear that the performances of sexual identities are pedagogical choices, and my experience has taught me the implications of a pedagogy in which heterosexuality is invoked as a tool of privilege in response to threat.

Although I initially framed this experience as a "failure" with a resistant student, conscious reflection and dialogue have enabled me to reposition my narrative of "failure" into a narrative of learning and future empowerment. Being part of a community, such as the TIGers, in which we examine our failures, are willing to see the hard truths of our practices, and improve our pedagogy can allow us to bring our expressed commitments to combating homophobia and heterosexism and our actions to do so into better alignment.

References

Athanases, S. Z., & Larrabee, T. G. (2003). Toward a consistent stance in teaching for equity: Learning to advocate for lesbian- and gay-identified youth. *Teaching and Teacher Education, 19*(2), 237–261.

Britzman, D. P., & Gilbert, J. (2004). What will have been said about gayness in teacher education? *Teaching Education, 15*(1), 81–96.

Chizhik, E. W., & Chizhik, A.W. (2005). Are you privileged or oppressed? Students' conceptions of themselves and others. *Urban Education, 40*(2), 116–143.

Clandinin, D. J., & Connelly, F. M. (2000). *Narrative inquiry: Experience and story in qualitative research*. San Francisco: Jossey-Bass.

Cochran-Smith, M. (2000). Blind vision: Unlearning racism in teacher education. *Harvard Educational Review, 70*(2), 157–190.

Cohen, H. S. (Producer), & Chasnoff, D. (Producer & Director). (1997). *It's elementary: Talking about gay issues in school* [Motion picture]. San Francisco: Women's Educational Media.

Coville, B. (1994). Am I blue? In M. D. Bauer (Ed.), *Am I blue? Coming out from the silence* (pp. 1–17). New York: HarperCollins.

Damico, A. M., & Quay, S. E. (2006). Stories of Boy Scouts, Barbie dolls, and prom dresses: Challenging college students to explore the popular culture of their childhood. *Teachers College Record, 108*(4), 604–620.

Davis, N. J. (1992). Teaching about inequality: Student resistance, paralysis, and rage. *Teaching Sociology, 20,* 232–238.

Deeb-Sossa, N., & Kane, H. (2007). "It's the Word of God": Students' resistance to questioning and overcoming heterosexism. *Feminist Teacher, 17*(2), 151–169.

Elhoweris, H., Parmeswaran, G., & Nemeldin, A. (2004). College students' myths about diversity and what college faculty can do. *Multicultural Education, 12*(2), 13–18.

Eyre, L. (1993). Compulsory heterosexuality in a university classroom. *Canadian Journal of Education, 18*(3), 273–284.

Fecho, B. (2000). Critical inquiries into language in an urban classroom. *Research in the Teaching of English, 34*(3), 368–395.

Fishman, S. M., & McCarthy, L. (2005). Talk about race: When student stories and multicultural curricula are not enough. *Race, Ethnicity, and Education, 8*(4), 347–364.

Focus on the Family. (2007). Focus on your child. Retrieved August 26, 2007, from http://www.focusonyourchild.com/hottopics/A0001284.cfm. Also available at http://www.qrd.org/religion/anti/FOF/focus.on.the.family-7.93

Freedman, E. B. (2007). Is teaching for social justice undemocratic? *Harvard Educational Review, 77*(4), 442–473.

Gardner, S., Dean, C., & McKaig, D. (1989). Responding to differences in the classroom: Responding to the politics of knowledge, class, and sexuality. *Sociology of Education, 62*(1), 64–74.

Goodman, D. J. (2000). Motivating people from privileged groups to support social justice. *Teachers College Record, 102*(6), 1061–1085.

Greene, M. (2003). In search of a critical pedagogy. In A. Darder, M. Baltodano, & R. D. Torres (Eds.), *The critical pedagogy reader* (pp. 97–112). New York: RoutledgeFalmer.

Griffin, P., & Ouellett, M. (2003). From silence to safety and beyond: Historical trends in addressing lesbian, gay, bisexual, transgender issues in K–12 schools. *Equity and Excellence in Education, 36*(2), 106–114.

Gutierrez-Gomez, C. (2002). Multicultural teacher preparation: Establishing safe environments for discussion of diversity issues. *Multicultural Education, 10*(1), 31–39.

hooks, b. (1994). *Teaching to transgress: Education as the practice of freedom.* New York: Routledge.

Kosciw, J. G. (2004). *The 2003 National School Climate Survey: The school-related experiences of our nation's lesbian, gay, bisexual, and transgender youth.* New York: GLSEN.

Kumashiro, K. K. (2004). Uncertain beginnings: Learning to teach paradoxically. *Theory into Practice, 43*(2), 111–115.

Ladson-Billings, G. (1996). Silences as weapons: Challenges of a Black professor teaching White students. *Theory into Practice, 35*(2), 79–85.

Leland, C. H., & Harste, J. C. (2005). Doing what we want to become: Preparing new urban teachers. *Urban Education, 40*(1), 60–77.

Maney, D. W., & Cain, R. E. (1997). Preservice elementary teachers' attitudes toward gay and lesbian parenting. *Journal of School Health, 67*(6), 236–241.

Marshall, P. L. (1999). Teachers' racial identity and the single course in multicultural education. *Action in Teacher Education, 20*(1), 59–69.

McIntosh, P. (1989). White privilege: Unpacking the invisible knapsack. *Peace and Freedom, 49*(4), 10–12.

McIntyre, A. (2002). Exploring Whiteness and multicultural education with prospective teachers. *Curriculum Inquiry, 32*(1), 31–49.

McLaren, P. (2003). Critical pedagogy: A look at the major concepts. In A. Darder, M. Baltodano, & R. D. Torres (Eds.), *The critical pedagogy reader* (pp. 69–96). New York: RoutledgeFalmer.

Milner, H. R. (2007). Race, narrative, and self-study in curriculum and teacher education. *Education and Urban Society, 39*(4), 584–609.

Robinson, K. H., & Ferfolja, T. (2001). "What are we doing this for?": Dealing with lesbian and gay issues in teacher education. *British Journal of Sociology of Education, 22*(2), 121–133.

Sharkey, J. (2004). Lives stories don't tell: Exploring the untold in autobiographies. *Curriculum Inquiry, 34*(4), 495–512.

Shipler, D. K. (1997). *A country of strangers: Blacks and Whites in America.* New York: Random House.

Shipler, D. K. (2004). *The working poor: Invisible in America.* New York: Knopf.

Sleeter, C. E. (2001). Preparing teachers for culturally diverse schools: Research and the overwhelming presence of whiteness. *Journal of Teacher Education, 52*(2), 94–106.

Solomon, R. P., Portelli, J. P., Daniel, B., & Campbell, A. (2005). The discourse of denial: How White teacher candidates construct race, racism, and "white privilege." *Race, Ethnicity, and Education, 8*(2), 147–169.

Stoddart, K. (1991). Lifestory: A device for dispersing authority in the introductory class. *Teaching Sociology, 19*(1), 70–73.

Sumara, D., & Davis, B. (1999). Interrupting heteronormativity: Toward a queer curriculum theory. *Curriculum Inquiry, 29*(2), 191–208.

Talburt, S. (2000). On not coming out, or, Reimagining limits. In W. J. Spurlin (Ed.), *Lesbian and gay studies and the teaching of English* (pp. 54–78). Urbana, IL: National Council of Teachers of English.

Tatum, B. D. (1992). Talking about race, learning about racism: The application of racial identity development theory in the classroom. *Harvard Educational Review, 62*(1), 1–24.

Vicars, M. (2006). Who are you calling queer? Sticks and stones may break my bones, but names will always hurt me. *British Educational Research Journal, 32*(3), 347–361.

Willis, A. I. (2003). Parallax: Addressing race in preservice literacy education. In S. Greene & D. Abt-Perkins (Eds.), *Making race visible: Literacy research for cultural understanding* (pp. 51–70). New York: Teacher College Press.

Winans, A. E. (2006). Queering pedagogy in the English classroom: Engaging with the places where thinking stops. *Pedagogy: Critical Approaches to Teaching Literature, Language, Composition, and Culture, 6*(1), 103–122.

Wood, L. (2005). *Not a Hetero*: Confessions of a dangerous homo. *Cultural Studies, 19*(4), 430–438.

3

Inquiring into Ally Work in Teacher Education

The Possibilities and Limitations of Textual Practice

CAROLINE T. CLARK

A S A WHITE, STRAIGHT TEACHER EDUCATOR in a large midwestern university, I have for 9 years now been teaching and reflectively studying my teaching of a very large, graduate, quarterlong course on issues of language, literacy, and culture to mostly White, straight, rural and suburban preservice teachers seeking certification in English, social studies, and multiple foreign languages. As I have studied this course, and my teaching of it, my lens has shifted; that is, what stands out for me has changed. Initially, my interest revolved around using narratives, particularly literacy narratives (e.g., Eldred & Mortenson, 1992), as a pedagogical tool. I believed that asking students to both write and read literacy narratives could play a role in shaping their understandings of literacy, pedagogy, and multiculturalism. At that time, my focus was "diversity" but with attention cast mainly on issues of race and ethnicity. And while the setting was my classroom, my primary questions were student-focused; my lens was cast on the students and how their understandings of literacy and multiculturalism were mediated through their reading and writing of particular kinds of texts (Clark & Medina, 2000).

In the intervening years, I have broadened the course, making space to address issues of gender, sexuality, homophobia, and heterosexism, and I have consciously worked to create tensions around what diversity means for educators. I have also actively repositioned myself in the class, moving from being a novice (which I was) and neutral (which I thought I was) instructor to becoming a clearly present advocate and ally, particularly for work against heterosexism and homophobia in classrooms and schools. Moreover, participating in the Pink TIGers has pushed me to look harder at myself in the mix of my classroom. Encouraged by my collaborators in the group, who so generously embrace risks, study themselves, and share their stories, I am reminded by Claudia Mitchell (2000) that "as teachers and teacher educators we need to be engaged in studying ourselves as part of our efforts to transform our own teaching" (p. 112) (see entry in the Annotated Bibliography of this book). This chapter is one attempt to examine myself in relation to my students and to question critically my goals for the course, my methods for working on these issues, and the key problems and possibilities I see for doing ally work through textual practices (Beavis, 2000) in teacher education. Ultimately, I discuss how what I have noticed through my teacher inquiry has helped me to rethink the possibilities and limitations of ally work through textual practice in teacher education.

The Teaching/Learning Context, or What I *Think* I'm Doing

The general focus of my long-term study has been a class known more by its course number (T&L 800) than its name—Introduction to Issues in Language, Literacy, and Culture." A very large class, the course assumes to provide secondary M.Ed. certification students with an introduction to key issues underlying their fields of study. While it is a required course, the framing and the content of the course have been left to my discretion, and I have taught the course every year but one since 1997.

While the course, across time, has included students who identify as lesbian or gay, including Lauren, who is now a member of the Pink TIGers and a contributor to this book (author of Chapter 4), the work that I describe here and that is a key focus of my inquiry involves educating straight preservice teachers about sexuality as part of "diversity" and encouraging them to see ally work on LGBT issues as a critical part of their jobs as teachers, regardless of content area or school context. The work of allies is often understood as straight people advocating for LGBT people. Based on this understanding, this work excludes my LGBT students. Indeed, in her critique of this chapter as the Pink TIGers prepared this manuscript, Lauren asked, "Is this work [ally work] only for straight people?" The response I would give is no. Ally work is about creating alliances across lines of difference—work that can and should be done by all teacher activists across identity categories or lines of difference. While my focus, here, is on ally work around sexuality, my stance, more generally, is that ally work is an important tool for working across many lines of difference—be these class, race, gender, ethnicity, or language—in an effort to marshal power and privilege from different sources to create a more socially just world, especially for young people in schools.

To trace the trajectories, logics, and textual practices of the course over time, and to examine my efforts to be an ally teaching against heterosexism and homophobia, I created a schematic view of my past nine syllabi for the course (see Table 3.1). Tracing my teaching work across the years, I looked to see how issues related to gender and sexuality were named, topically, and I looked to see how texts—including film and print-based media—were positioned, produced, and taken up in the course. A persistent assumption of mine has been a belief that narratives—both written and read—can serve as "powerful tools in coming to understand literacy, multiculturalism, ourselves and one another in a diverse society" (Clark & Medina, 2000, p. 64; Dyson & Genishi, 1994). I believe that social realities and concepts such as literacy, gender, and sexuality are not given, but are "meanings that we achieve by the sharing of human cognition" (Bruner, 1986, p. 122). Through language (be it spoken, written, nonverbal actions, or other semiotic systems) these understandings are "discoursed into being" (Bloome et al., 2005). My goals for the course are expressed consistently in my syllabi across the years:

> Students in this course will be encouraged to take a critical stance toward current issues and debates presented in both a larger lecture/discussion format and within smaller breakout groups led by graduate teaching assistants. Students will engage in large lecture/discussions of the broader definitions, issues, and perspectives and then, in smaller groups, address particular issues as they are manifested in various teaching contexts in which they are working. In order to contextualize these theoretical and pedagogical issues, we will read a variety of "literacy narratives," written from multiple perspectives, and use these to frame our understandings of language, literacy and culture more generally. (T&L 800 Syllabus, Autumn 2006)

TABLE 3.1. Syllabi Analysis Table

Theme	Personal Narratives	"Theory-Based" Narratives	"Co-constructed" Narratives
1997	*Wild Meat and the Bully Burgers* by Lois Ann Yamanaka *Push* by Sapphire	"Silencing in Public Schools" by Michele Fine "Creative Maladjustment and the Struggle for Public Education" by Herbert Kohl	Reading Log (Written) 3 Paper Sequence: Defining Literacy Essay, Personal Literacy Narrative, Literacy & Pedagogy Essay (Written) Ongoing Class Discussion (Oral) Mid-Term & Final Course Evaluations (Written) Final Analytic Paper (Written)
1998	*Wild Meat and the Bully Burgers* by Lois Ann Yamanaka *Rivethead* by Ben Hamper	"Creative Maladjustment and the Struggle for Public Education" by Herbert Kohl	Personal Literacy Narrative (Written) Interview Across Difference (Written) Ongoing Class Discussion (Oral) Multicultural Curriculum Guide (Written) Mid-Term & Final Course Evaluations (Written)
1999 "Gender Issues"		"A Historical Perspective on Gender" by Elizabeth St. Pierre "Wimpy Boys and Macho Girls: Gender Equity at the Crossroads" by L. J. McClure "A Rationale and Unit Plan for Introducing Gay and Lesbian Literature into the Grade Twelve Curriculum" by Robert Hammett	Personal Literacy Narrative (Written) Interview Across Difference (Written) Ongoing Class Discussion (Oral) Unit Plan (Written) Mid-Term & Final Course Evaluations (Written)
2000 "Gender & Youth Culture"	*Speak* by Laurie Halse Anderson	"A Historical Perspective on Gender" by Elizabeth St. Pierre "Wimpy Boys and Macho Girls: Gender Equity at the Crossroads" by L. J. McClure "A Rationale and Unit Plan for Introducing Gay and Lesbian Literature into the Grade Twelve Curriculum" by Robert Hammett	Personal Literacy Narrative (Written) Ongoing Class Discussion (Oral) Unit Plan (Written) Mid-term & Final Course Evaluations (Written) Becoming an ESL Learner (Oral) Issues Analysis (Written)

TABLE 3.1. Syllabi Analysis Table *(continued)*

Theme	Personal Narratives	"Theory-Based" Narratives	"Co-constructed" Narratives
2001 "**Gender and Sexuality**"	"Language of Violence" by the Disposable Heroes of Hiphoprisy "What Are Homosexuals For?" by Andrew Sullivan	"The Missing Discourse About Gender and Sexuality in the Social Studies" by Margaret Crocco	Personal Literacy Narrative (Written) Ongoing Class Discussion (Oral) Unit Plan (Written) Mid-Term & Final Course Evaluations (Written)
2002 "**Gender, Sexuality, and GLBTQ Youths & Teachers**"	*It's Elementary* [Video] "Language of Violence" by the Disposable Heroes of Hiphoprisy	"The Missing Discourse About Gender and Sexuality in the Social Studies" by Margaret Crocco "Wimpy Boys and Macho Girls: Gender Equity at the Crossroads" by L.J. McClure "What Difference Does It Make? The Story of a Lesbian Teacher" by Carla Rensenbrink "Young Adult Reflections on Having an Openly Gay Teacher During Early Adolescence" by Eric Rofes	Personal Literacy Narrative (Written) Ongoing Class Discussion (Oral) Issues Analysis (Written) K-W-L: Gender & Sexuality (Oral/Written) Unit Plan (Written) Mid-Term & Final Course Evaluations (Written)
2003 "**Gender, Sexuality, and GLBTQ Youths & Teachers**"	*It's Elementary* [Video]	"The Missing Discourse About Gender and Sexuality in the Social Studies" by Margaret Crocco "What Difference Does It Make? The Story of a Lesbian Teacher" by Carla Rensenbrink "Young Adult Reflections on Having an Openly Gay Teacher During Early Adolescence" by Eric Rofes	Personal Literacy Narrative (Written) Ongoing Class Discussion (Oral) Unit Plan (Written) Unpacking Knapsack of Privilege (Written) Mid-Term & Final Course Evaluations (Written)

TABLE 3.1. Syllabi Analysis Table (*continued*)

Theme	Personal Narratives	"Theory-Based" Narratives	"Co-constructed" Narratives
2005 "Gender, Sexuality, & LGBT Youths & Teachers"	*It's Elementary* [Video] Jane Elliott Lecture, "The Anatomy of Prejudice"	"The Missing Discourse About Gender and Sexuality in the Social Studies" by Margaret Crocco "What Difference Does It Make? The Story of a Lesbian Teacher" by Carla Rensenbrink "'Dickheads, Wuses, and Faggots': Addressing Issues of Masculinity and Homophobia in the Critical Literacy Classroom" by Will Martino	Personal Literacy Narrative (Written) Weekly Response Papers (Written) Unpacking Knapsack of Privilege (Written) Ongoing Class Discussion (Oral) Unit Plan (Written) Pedagogic Creed (Written) Mid-Term & Final Course Evaluations (Written)
2006 "Gender, Sexuality, & LGBT Youths & Teachers"	*It's Elementary* [Video] "Youth Video Outreach" (Film and Panel Discussion with Local LGBT Youth) "Am I Blue?" by Bruce Coville *Covering: The Hidden Assault on Our Civil Rights* by Kenji Yoshino	"The Missing Discourse About Gender and Sexuality in the Social Studies" by Margaret Crocco "Disrupting Dichotomies for Social Change: A Review of, Critique of, and Complement to Current Educational Literacy Scholarship on Gender" by Mollie V. Blackburn *Covering: The Hidden Assault on Our Civil Rights* by Kenji Yoshino	Personal Literacy Narrative (Written) 4 Response Papers/Quizzes with Explicit Prompts (Written) Unpacking Knapsack of Privilege (Written) Ongoing Class Discussion (Oral) Unit Plan (Written) Position Paper on the Role of Schools in Challenging vs. Maintaining the Status Quo (Written) Mid-Term & Final Course Evaluations (Written)

Framing these somewhat generic goals are my beliefs and assumptions regarding what it means to "take a critical stance."

Mary Louise Pratt (1991) describes teaching in "the contact zones." Here, classrooms hold the potential to become "social spaces where cultures meet, clash, and grapple with each other, often in contexts of highly asymmetrical relations of power" (p. 34). In effect, Pratt is calling for the enactment of a critical pedagogy (Freire, 1970; Shor, 1980, 1992) and the creation of spaces where teachers and students inquire, together, into issues that are central to their lives and worlds. These issues, then, reflect a set of purposes and practices that hold the potential to bond a classroom together in a kind of community while honoring the differences of the individuals within the group.

Examining Myself and My Students, or Taking Notice

In taking a systematic look at myself in relation to my students as part of my efforts to transform my own teaching, I've noticed some things. In part, what I've noticed is rooted in "textual practice," that is, the reading, writing, and discussing work that my students and I do together, and issues of "how texts are read, and ask to be read" (Beavis, 2000). In addition, what I've noticed relates to a distinction between what I'm calling ally work and anti work. I draw this distinction based on my experiences in teaching this course across time, as well as my readings on antiracist education (e.g., Gillborn, 1995; Thompson, 1997, 2003), gay-straight alliances (Miceli, 2005), and the work that heterosexuals can do in support of gay rights (e.g., Ayres & Brown, 2005; DiStefano et al., 2000; Evans & Broido, 2005). Anti work serves primarily to interrupt racist, heterosexist, and homophobic discourses. Ally work, on the other hand, moves beyond interrupting racist, heterosexist, and homophobic discourses; rather, ally work invites critical dialogue and discussion, interrogating perceived lines of difference and inquiring into the possibilities for creating productive alliances across these lines. In the remainder of this chapter, I will explore what I mean by ally work in the context of this course. Drawing on my analysis of classroom texts and syllabi and data collected from students in recent years, I'll highlight some of the key things I have noticed in my students and myself—parallels I see between their willingness and sense of possibility for doing anti work and ally work, and my own struggles in doing similar work through this course itself.

Data discussed here were collected in spring and early summer 2006, following the 2005–2006 academic year, and in autumn 2006, near the outset of the 2006–2007 academic year. English language arts (ELA) preservice teachers in the 2005–2006 cohort completed surveys at the conclusion of all course work and student teaching ($N = 35$). In addition, seven students from this cohort self-selected to participate in individual and group interviews in late spring and early summer, following their final quarter of student teaching. Just over half of the students in the autumn 2006 section of T&L 800 chose to complete the same survey at the beginning of their 2006–2007 coursework ($N = 40$). In addition, students from this course elected to share their papers (19/76) and their responses to reading prompts (65/76) for further analysis.

My Textual Practices

Silence

The first thing I noticed in reviewing the course textual practices was silence. For 2 years (1997 and 1998) I was completely silent on issues of gender, sexuality, homophobia, and heterosexism. I did not name these issues as themes in my course syllabus explicitly, nor did I raise them directly as topics related to the narratives read, written, and shared in the course. Looking back, I am astonished by my failure to take notice of issues and opportunities that were clearly present. In my early years of teaching this class—and determining what "belonged" in a course focused on issues of language, literacy and culture—I felt certain and safe in discussing race, class, and ethnicity. All these seemed relevant, and all were addressed in the texts at hand. What I failed to notice, however, was "the presence of absence" (Mitchell, 2000). Despite my initial use of texts that explicitly take up questions of gender and sexuality—particularly the works of Yamanaka, Sapphire, and Hamper—these issues were noticeably absent by name in my syllabi. (Nowhere, in either my course assignments or my syllabi, do I explicitly name gender or sexuality as a category of concern). And while I consistently invite students to "select a slice of your life, and examine it in some detail" (personal literacy narrative assignment, Autumn 1997) or to respond to "the relationship between the character's experiences with literacy learning, language, and culture and your own experiences" (reading log and reading group participation guidelines, Autumn 1997), I never direct students explicitly to take up or take on issues of gender and sexuality. I find this startling in part because the very presence of the student body—and the students' bodies—was a presence that was absent. Students, male and female, gay, straight, and bisexual, all were present in my classroom. And yet I failed to see them embodied as such, instead maintaining a stringently limited focus on race, ethnicity, and language, and seeing these as the primary issues in the course. Even as we read Michele Fine's (1987) "Silencing in Public Schools," and even as I asked my students to consider silencing around issues of race, I failed to interrogate my own silence around gender and sexuality.

Trying to Get It Right

Another key issue I noticed from looking at this course and myself across the years is my desire to "get it right." By *get it right*, I mean, in part, my desire to move students toward a particular mindset, while also being open to change myself. In working toward both these goals, I have felt frustrated and less than open. Yes, I claim to value multiple perspectives; I want my students to critically consider issues from many sides. But I also want them to end up somewhere—somewhere quite specific, in fact. I want them to move into the world as educators who will combat racism, sexism, homophobia, and heterosexism in their classrooms and in the world. I want them to accept and affirm LGBTQ and non-gender-conforming students, colleagues, and parents. I want them to embrace these values strongly—and then teach them and reinforce them in school-age children like my 9-year-old daughter and her currently kind, accepting, inquisitive peers.

The urgency I feel in achieving these goals increases when I read the GLSEN annual school climate surveys (Kosciw, Diaz, & Greytak, 2008) (see entry in the Annotated Bibliography of this book) and is compounded, each year, by the feedback I receive from students. Never mind the 75 students who say they have loved, learned from, or been challenged by the course. Instead, I find I focus on the handful of students who resisted the course, always adapting the course to try to change the minds of these particular students. Witness, for example, a comment on an end-of-course evaluation from one of my students in 1998:

> I resist . . . many of the readings. They assert that blacks or women must be treated different than everyone else. . . . I feel that Gilyard and some aspects of this class attempt to re-enforce these norms in an attempt to justify the lack of success. This is obviously political and I feel it is my duty as an educator to prevent politics from inhibiting the education of my students. Progress is the key, not political ambition. Although my conclusions differ somewhat from the articles and class discussion, I have engaged the readings and

thought deeply about the issues. I have put myself in the shoes of others long before this class and during. I have not resisted this class, I have simply derived different conclusions and I am thankful that in America, I can still think independently without punishment. (White male, final evaluation)

My response the next year, in autumn quarter 1999, was to name gender explicitly and to add more readings that locate gender historically—moves designed to respond to my former students' comments. Likewise, after teaching Lauren in this course in 2001, and hearing how the course was experienced by her as a lesbian student of teaching, I revised yet again, naming even more explicitly the topics of "gender, sexuality, and GLBTQ youths and teachers" as issues that fit under my umbrella of "language, literacy, and culture," and adding more readings and videos to address and name these commitments.

Students' Responses

In looking at the most recent versions of this course, and my students' responses to it, I see some productive evolution, some possibility that I might actually be doing the right things—problematic as this drive toward "rightness" is. While studies on ally work in education are limited, and seem to focus more on issues of higher education, student services, and counseling, the literature consistently points to the positive impact of exposing students to guest speakers, panels, and films that present the experiences and perspectives of LGBT people, and the critical importance of engaging students in explicit work on naming and acknowledging unearned privilege relative to race, class, gender and sexuality (see, e.g., DeStefano et al., 2000; Evans & Broido, 2005). Both these forms of textual practice have been features of my course, and in the autumn 2006 version of T&L 800, one of the highlights of the quarter was a screening of a youth-made film, *20 Straws* (see entry in Annotated Bibliography of this book), documenting the experiences of Central Ohio LGBT youth, followed by a panel discussion with the young videographers (Gjestvang & Youth Video OUTreach, 2006).

In addition, the literature on ally work often suggests drawing on "heterosexual identity development" models (many of which are premised on White racial development models) in order to understand how students grow into being socially just allies (see, e.g., DeStefano et al., 2000; Evans & Broido, 2005).

Scholars like Audrey Thompson (1997, 2003), who focus on antiracist work, however, raise concerns for me around the ways such models center Whiteness and focus on creating "good Whites." She problematizes these models, along with general work attending to White privilege, because they suggest some idealized, developmental "end" that we, as teacher educators, will recognize in our students once it is achieved. Moreover, she suggests that much work on addressing privilege—particularly White privilege—turns into efforts at assuaging White guilt, once again positioning Whiteness—or in this case, straightness—at the center of anti work.

A close look at the some of the course writings and interviews with students points to continued tensions between ally work, anti work, and what I'm currently calling "neutrality." A *neutral position* is one in which the student names his or her privileges, relative to race, gender, language or sexuality, but does not move beyond simple identification. There is no analysis of the implications or consequences of unearned privilege, and no responses or actions are suggested in terms of teaching. In one case, a response is suggested, but it is framed in deficit terms, suggesting that teachers will need to be aware that students who lack certain privileges will face greater challenges. An *anti position* is one in which students name privileges, but frame their responses in terms of guilt, in effect centering Whiteness and straightness, and framing their responses in ways that position them as "good" examples of White, straight people (Thompson, 2003). In these papers, privilege may be identified and analyzed as systemic, and students express a desire to work against racism, heterosexism, and homophobia, but their responses to issues of privilege are framed individually. In describing ways of responding as teachers, for example, students focused on responding personally to individual students who may not hold the same privileges they do. Finally, an *ally position* is one in which students both named their unearned privileges and described the obligations of privilege. In these papers, students analyzed privilege relative to systemic issues of race, class, gender, and sexuality and framed their response through a similar lens. As teachers, they saw a need to respond to systems of oppression and to make their students aware of these systems. Table 3.2 provides illustrative quotes from course papers and interviews to further exemplify the nature of these three positions. Of the 19 papers collected, all were written by White students who self-identified as straight. In terms of the positions forwarded by students in these papers, eight articulated neutral positions, seven articulated anti positions, and four articulated ally positions.

TABLE 3.2. Autumn 2006 Paper Response Positions

Neutral	Considered altogether, my background was full of unearned privileges which helped to equip me for relative ease and success. Many students do not have these privileges, and being a good teacher will require that I recognize challenges that others face that I did not have to, and that I help students use what they have in order to succeed. –White, Female, Social Studies, Straight Those people like myself who have many of the invisible privileges do not notice them because we do not take the time to think about what it would be like in someone else's situation, therefore our invisible privileges remain invisible to us. As a preservice teacher I have learned that it requires this effort of acknowledging such privileges and the opportunities that come with them to actually learn about our students and understand what they bring to our classrooms. If we use our knowledge to provide everyone with such opportunities, then all of our students will be privileged, even if only in our classrooms. —White, Female, Foreign Language, Straight As a social studies teacher, I feel as though it is important to teach the students about race issues that have plagued the world. I grew up in a family who was tolerant of other races and ethnicities so it is hard for me to relate to someone who has a hatred for another based on the color of their skin. With that in mind, I will not try to attempt to change my students if they have these views. … As a teacher, I find it is important to keep my personal feelings regarding a particular issue to myself. We have been talking about non-biased teaching in our social studies methods class —Angela, White, Female, Social Studies, Straight
Anti	After realizing the significant educational, social, and daily benefits that I receive merely by being white and straight, I have a newfound respect for all types of minorities. As a future teacher, I also hope to follow McIntosh's challenge that "describing white privilege makes one newly accountable" (p. 135). I hope to foster a classroom atmosphere where all students feel included and encouraged to learn by choosing materials that include all types of minorities, demanding all students to respect each other, and facilitating discussion about such issues as social inequality. Finally, I believe that the foreign language classroom is an especially effective place for teaching students to examine their own assumptions about culture and language. In this way, I plan to help my students learn to question the established social inequalities and respect people who are different from themselves. –White, Female, Foreign Language, Straight Nevertheless, there are many people who are suffering as a result of my privileges; and this may be a subconscious reason for my desire to become a

TABLE 3.2. Autumn 2006 Paper Response Positions (*continued*)

Anti (*continued*)	teacher. I would experience great pride if I could help to even the odds for some of my students who did not have the same unearned privileges that I have. –White, Female, Social Studies, Straight Teaching students to be accepting of homosexuality, and to see men and women as equals is not part of the normal realm of teaching. I do believe that it is very important to stop students from using derogatory language in classes. No one should be calling other students "fags" or "sissies" in class, as that is disrespectful to both teacher and classmates. I will stop students from using sexual slurs because I want to have an inviting and safe classroom. However, I do not believe that teachers should correct students' thoughts about homosexuality and misogyny. —David, White, Male, Social Studies, Straight
Ally	Being aware of one's own invisible privileges in society and recognizing that they inherently disadvantage others is not enough for a teacher. Instead, educators must actively combat these disadvantages in their classrooms through maintaining high efficacy, offering extra time and attention towards those in need, and by reading texts that challenge normative notions of gender and sexuality while insisting on a safe, respectful and gay-friendly environment. –White, Female, English, Straight Though I was given many assets that I did not earn, I can use them to trouble the system that creates this advantage. Only by educating others and bringing awareness to the topics of LGBTQ rights, language assumptions, and economic privilege can any change ensue. The may require me to lay down my privileges, but I feel that if it means that I will still be an equal with others, it is not necessary to fight against it. I look forward to my knapsack being lighter in the future. —White, Female, English, Straight …confronting bigotry in the classroom is not about pushing one's own agenda, but about educating the many students who may be ignorant of the various facets of the issues that they had not previously considered. The Blackburn article then helped me see realistic ways I can confront these issues in my future English classroom via the curriculum. . . . English teachers, such as I hope to be, can fight outward bigotry by exposing students to texts that disrupt their notions of marginalized social groups in America. If students still choose to be bigoted even after classroom attempts to educate them about social injustices, then that is their prerogative. However, this will not stop me from continually confronting the ignorance of their racist, sexist, or homophobic values via a diverse curriculum. —White, Female, English, Straight

Limitations of Ally Work Through
Teacher Education and Textual Practice

In looking across my textual practices as a teacher educator over the years, and my students' responses to these practices, I see several parallel tensions and problematic assumptions that I believe are worth examining. In looking at my own moves, and analyzing my students' positions as neutral, anti, and ally, I see similarities to my own positions, of silence, of trying to get things right and, in my continued interrogation of the paradoxes involved in both teaching for social justice and social change while being open to diverse perspectives and opinions.

As I have indicated above, one of my textual practices across the years has been to add texts in order to address concerns of students and counter my own silences. Indeed, I think my initial silences on issues could (generously, perhaps) be interpreted as trying to be neutral. Like my neutral students, I was naming issues and privileges relative to these—around race, language, gender, and finally, more explicitly, sexuality—but my practices did not move beyond simple identification and moving through a litany of themes/topics. Over time, and in response, I added texts (including books, articles, films, and finally guest speakers) in an effort to get things right. While I do not dispute the value of these additions, I do find the motivations oddly paradoxical. For one, I often feel that I am "teaching backward." Each year, the course is revised in response to former students; each year I find that I am looking backward in order to move forward. Moreover, across the years, my syllabus is simply bursting at the seams with new readings. Here, again, I find that I am perpetually seeking the right text that will finally move my students to the place where I want them to be, especially with regard to teaching against heterosexism and homophobia. What I find interesting—and worrisome—in my teaching toward these outcomes are my assumptions that (1) this goal is achievable and desirable and (2) I will achieve this goal through texts.

In comparing myself with my students, again, I see parallels between those who take an anti stance and my own desires to get things right as a teacher educator. I had much in common with my anti students, who named privileges but framed their responses in terms of guilt, centering Whiteness and straightness and positioning themselves as "good" examples of White, straight people (Thompson, 2000): My responses were aimed at maintaining my position as a good, nice, well-liked professor who, while committed to issues of social justice, did not push students too hard. My ambivalence in pushing my students harder was a sort of not trying to "rock the boat" (to quote a 1st-year teacher's position on how he might combat heterosexism and homophobia in schools). I wanted to work on homophobia and heterosexism, but I still wanted to be open (read, "neutral"). In many ways, I was a bit like David (see Table 3.2)—saying that I would make my students aware of the issues, but I would not directly challenge them because I needed to stay open. I wanted to continue to be a good (White, straight) teacher and to stay seen as such in the eyes of my students.

Without a doubt, though, my hope as a teacher educator has been to get it right. For me, another part of getting it right means to prepare students who will move into the world of teaching with all the caring and compassion they can muster for all the many students and families they will encounter. Of course I want them to be knowledgeable, in terms of content and pedagogy. But I also want them to understand the limits of what they know and can know about an "other" (Bernstein, 1992) so as to be open to learning from students and their families. In attempting to achieve these goals, I have bumped headlong into what many others seem already to know: getting it right in teaching is impossible, and if it were possible, then it would not be teaching. Elizabeth Ellsworth (1997) captures this paradox in her discussion of teaching as "a performative event that is unrepeatable" (p. 159)—a stance that is significantly different from my problematic approach of attempting to get students to "occupy and repeat the same social and political position occupied" by me (p. 160). Rather, Ellsworth suggests that "teaching about and across difference without driving toward or prizing assimilation or the sameness of understanding requires an ability to allow plural worlds to exist side by side" (p. 174).

While I believe and value Ellsworth's position, it worries me nonetheless. How can work against heterosexism and homophobia get done through teacher education if discourses of heteronormativity are allowed to stay intact as simply "plural worlds" that exist "side by side"? Kumashiro (2001), Villanueva (1997), and others help me to imagine possibilities beyond an "I'm okay, you're okay" approach to teacher preparation. Like Ellsworth, Kumashiro sees teaching as a paradoxical, performative act, noting that "the teacher cannot control how the student reads what the teacher is trying to en-act" (2001, p. 46). He goes on:

> There is always a space between the teaching and the learning, and rather than try to close that space (and control where and how the student is changed), the teacher should work within that space, embrace that paradox, and explore the possibilities of disruptions and change that reside

within the unknowable (Lather, 1998). . . . We are not trying to *move to a better place*; rather we are just trying *to move*. . . . Although we do not want to *be* (the same), we also do not want to *be better* (since any utopian vision would simply be a different and foretold way *to be*, and thus, a different way to be stuck in reified sameness); rather, we want to *constantly become*, we want difference, change, newness. And this change cannot come if we close off the space-between. (p. 46)

Embracing paradox and working in the space between teaching and learning makes me hopeful. I am encouraged by the possibility of movement and the potential for breaking out of the status quo. I would be lying, however, if I did not also recognize the vulnerability of working in that space. My urge to get it right is a strong one, and it belies my named commitment to a critical stance. If I am committed to moving my students toward a critical stance, then I need to take one myself—I need to make my classroom a true space of critical inquiry, a space where, as Bob Fecho argues, "the sheer unknowns of the inquiry leave all participants open to potential pain and struggle" (2001, p. 33). As Fecho asserts, and I agree, "It seems insensitive to ask learners to interrogate their own stances as well as the stances of the institutions and others around them without understanding that these learners might feel threatened by the activity" (p. 33).

So, what about textual practice? As I noted earlier, I see all the work in this course, be it the reading of narratives, the viewing of films and videos, or the co-construction of narratives through discussion and writing, as textual practice. As Catherine Beavis (2000) notes in her work on young people reading/playing video games, "All textual practice, including reading, writing and discussion, engages questions of representation, negotiation and positioning—issues to do with how texts are read, and ask to be read; with (re)presentation of self, with ideology and with identity" (para. 5). Through my self-analysis and student data, I have attempted to show this work of representation, negotiation, and positioning relative to the key positions I noticed in the course—of neutral/silence; anti/getting it right; and ally work. However, as my bloated syllabi show, I have tried to make texts do the work of teaching. I have assumed that I could find the right texts to meet any challenge—and that I could control how these texts are read (Kumashiro, 2000; Ellsworth, 1997).

Likewise—and perhaps like it or not—as teachers, we get taken up as "texts" (Talburt, 2000) (see entry in the Annotated Bibliography of this book). As the lesbian university professor in Susan Talburt's study asserts of students, "They know when you have certain things in mind, and it limits what they're going to do. It also limits what you do, so you can't be active in relation to what they're saying, and let it push you, then nothing you say is going to push them" (p. 69). "Olivia," the subject of Talburt's study, works to destabilize and unfix her identity in her classroom so that she is not limited to speaking for or from some reified identity category. I question the possibility of this stance, and Talburt points out its paradoxes for Olivia. Even in working that unknowable space between teaching and learning, I cannot deny my presence in the classroom. To pretend that my presence, power, and interests do not matter would, in fact, be to privilege them by *not* acknowledging them—by allowing myself to not stand in the fray and be open to change. To continue to look for the right text would be to deny the presence of myself as a text and limit the possibilities of textual practice as a space for (re)presentation—as a space to constantly become.

What I'm Working on Now

I am working now to continue making this class a space of possibility. To do this, I know that I need to give up my desire to "get it right" and my search for the perfect text. As frustrating as these habits are, they are also comfortable; I am used to the struggle to get it right. But as Bob Fecho (2001) points out, "Those who work with various forms of inquiry-based pedagogy have to resist the reflex to seek a too-easily-won comfort and instead . . . embrace that which feels threatening, open it to investigation, and learn from the process" (p. 33). Which brings me to ally work, and my current point in this ongoing teacher inquiry. Like my few students who have embraced an ally stance in my course, I see parallels to where I am now, as a teacher educator working for change. I think my frustration with my own anti stance is part of what leads me to take a stronger ally stance. In these past 2 years, I know I have directly challenged my students more. I have named my commitments much more clearly. I have required students to participate in activities that will expose them more directly to LGBT people and their issues and that will force them to address their own homophobia and heterosexism. I know that this has made me unpopular with some of my students (and adversely, perhaps more popular with others). But I think my motivation has shifted significantly from my anti position of wanting to get it right but still be "neutral." I know I am not neutral on these issues—and my students know it. I know, too, that I have much, much more work to do. I need to model more—as my students indicate. I also need to be careful. I don't want to create more resistance through my work; on the other hand, I do not think I am "making" my students more heterosexist and homophobic. I believe that their responses (either positive or negative) are rooted in their already held beliefs and that part of what I do through my teaching is simply to bring these more into the light and allow them to flourish (for better or worse). My hope is that most of this work is for the better—that my students see that social justice work and work against heterosexism and homophobia can and should occur in schools and as part of teaching. And, indeed, that my students who do not bring these values understand that their intolerance does not belong in schools.

References

Ayres, I., & Brown, J. G. (2005). *Straightforward: How to mobilize heterosexual support for gay rights*. Princeton, NJ: Princeton University Press.

Beavis, C. (2000). Popular culture, textual practice, and identity: Literacy and new technologies in the middle years of schooling. *Annual conference, the Australian Association for Research in Education*, http://www.aare.edu.au/00pap/bea00495.htm

Bernstein, R. (1992). *The new constellation: The ethical-political horizons of modernity/postmodernity*. Cambridge, MA: MIT Press.

Bloome, D., Carter, S. P., Christian, B. M., Madrid, S., Otto, S., Shuart-Faris, N., & Smith, M. (2005). *On discourse analysis in classrooms: Approaches to language and literacy research*. New York: Teachers College Press.

Bruner, J. (1986). *Actual minds, possible worlds*. Cambridge, MA: Harvard University Press.

Bruner, J. (1994). Life as narrative. In A. H. Dyson & C. Genishi (Eds.), *The need for story: Cultural diversity in classroom and community* (pp. 28–37). Urbana, IL: National Council of Teachers of English.

Clark, C. T., & Medina, C. L. (2000). How reading and writing literacy narratives affects pre-service teachers' understandings of literacy, pedagogy, and multiculturalism. *Journal of Teacher Education, 51*(1), 63–76.

DiStefano, T. M., Croteau, J. M., Anderson, M. Z., Kampa-Kokesch, S., & Bullard, M. A. (2000). Experiences of being heterosexual allies to lesbian, gay, and bisexual people: A qualitative exploration. *Journal of College Counseling, 3*, 131–140.

Dyson, A. H., & Genishi, C. (Eds.). (1994). *The need for story: Cultural diversity in classroom and community*. Urbana, IL: National Council of Teachers of English.

Eldred, J. C., & Mortensen, P. (1992). Reading literacy narratives. *College English, 54*(5), 521–539.

Ellsworth, E. (1997). *Teaching positions: Difference, pedagogy, and the power of address*. New York: Teachers College Press.

Evans, N. J., & Broido, E. M. (2005). Encouraging the development of social justice attitudes and actions in heterosexual students. *New Directions for Student Services, 110,* 43–54.

Fecho, B. (2001). "Why are you doing this?": Acknowledging and transcending threat in a critical inquiry classroom. *Research in the Teaching of English, 36*(1), 9–37.

Fine, M. (1987). Silencing in public schools. *Language Arts, 64*(2), 157–174.

Freire, P. (1970). *Pedagogy of the oppressed.* New York: Continuum.

Gillborn, D. (1995). *Racism and antiracism in real schools.* London: Open University Press.

Gjestvang, L., & Youth Video OUTreach Collective. (Producer & Director). (2007). *20 straws: Growing up gay* [Motion Picture]. Available from http://videooutreach.org/

Kosciw, J. G., Diaz, E. M., & Greytak, E. A. (2008). *The 2007 National School Climate Survey: The experiences of lesbian, gay, bisexual, and transgender youth in our nation's schools.* New York: GSLEN.

Kumashiro, K. K. (2000). Toward a theory of anti-oppressive education. *Review of Educational Research, 70*(1), 25–54.

Kumashiro, K. K. (2001). "Posts" perspectives on anti-oppressive education in social studies, English, mathematics, and science classrooms. *Educational Researcher, 30*(3), 3–12.

Miceli, M. (2005). *Standing out, standing together: The social and political impact of gay-straight alliances.* New York: Routledge.

Michaels, S. (1999, Spring). Stories in contact: Teacher research in the academy. *ADE Bulletin, 122,* 59–64.

Mitchell, C. (2000). "What's out there?" Gay and lesbian literature for children and young adults. In W. J. Spurlin (Ed.), *Lesbian and gay studies and the teaching of English: Positions, pedagogies, and cultural politics* (pp. 112–130). Urbana, IL: National Council of Teachers of English.

Pratt, M. L. (1991). Arts of the contact zone. *Profession, 91*(1), 33–40.

Shor, I. (1980). *Critical teaching and everyday life.* Chicago: University of Chicago Press.

Shor, I. (1992). *Empowering education: Critical teaching for social change.* Chicago: University of Chicago Press.

Talburt, S. (2000). On not coming out; or, Reimagining limits. In W. J. Spurlin (Ed.), *Lesbian and gay studies and the teaching of English: Positions, pedagogies, and cultural politics* (pp. 54–78). Urbana, IL: National Council of Teachers of English.

Thompson, A. (1997). For: Anti-racist education. *Curriculum Inquiry, 27*(1), 7–44.

Thompson, A. (2003). Tiffany, friend of people of color: White investments in anti-racism. *Qualitative Studies in Education, 16*(1), 7–29.

Villanueva, Jr., V. (1997). Shoot-out at the I'm OK, You're OK corral. In J. F. Trimmer (Ed.), *Narration as knowledge: Tales of the teaching life* (pp. 43–50). Portsmouth, NH: Boynton/Cook/Heinemann.

4

Being Out and Reading Queer-Inclusive Texts in a High School English Classroom

LAUREN M. KENNEY

M Y WORK AGAINST HETEROSEXISM and homophobia in school has evolved dramatically since my 1st year of teaching. As a lesbian, I encountered homophobia and heterosexism throughout my Master of Education program and realized that I needed to do something to prevent my future students from being the targets or perpetrators of this hatred.

Initially, I decided that the solution was to be out in my classroom. Knowing a gay person would surely change my students' homophobic attitudes. The end. I didn't need to use queer-inclusive texts in my class. Eventually, it became clear that while being out did seem to help, it was insufficient. Over time, I realized that fear was preventing me from doing important work, such as teaching texts by and about queer people, and I began doing more. I joined the Pink TIGers to find support as I moved to take more action against homophobia and heterosexism in school. I incorporated queer-inclusive texts into my 9th-grade curriculum, beginning with texts that included gay and lesbian characters and ultimately introducing texts that included transgender characters, invited interested students to a book group that met at a center for LGBTQ youth to discuss queer-inclusive texts, and started a gay-straight alliance (GSA) that was active both in and out of school.

The first part of this chapter is about being an out teacher and the effects on me, my students, and the school climate. The second part is about reading queer-inclusive texts in class and its impact on students' attitudes about LGBTQ people and issues.

I'm Coming Out, So You Better Get This Party Started[1]

I decided to come out in my classroom during my M.Ed. program. Although I'd been out for 5 years, I closeted myself at the start of the program, fearing that I would not get a job as an out lesbian.

As a student, I took Caroline Clark's Introduction to Issues in Language, Literacy, and Culture course for preservice teachers—the 800 class she writes about in Chapter 3. The last week of October, the focus was gender and sexuality. I looked forward to that day, thinking I would learn what I was in for as a lesbian educator. We read four texts prior to class, two about gender and two about sexuality. One of the texts was the Disposable Heroes of Hiphoprisy rap "Language of Violence" (Franti, 1992), about a 15-year-old student who is beaten to death by a group of boys who perceive him to be gay. I was drawn to it as a text I might use with students, but I was also frustrated by it. Wouldn't most agree that murdering someone—regardless of his or her sexuality—is wrong? What about the less egregious manifestations of homophobia that LGBTQ students and teachers face day to day in school? Moreover, it ends with a violent homosexual rape that's portrayed as the perpetrator's just desserts. The second text was an article by the gay White conservative Andrew Sullivan titled, "What Are Homosexuals For?" In it, Sullivan seeks to demystify gays for a straight audience. He asserts that, as a gay man, he has noticed that many stereotypes about gay people are true, but qualifies his argument by admitting that this may be a generalization. I was infuriated by his presumptuousness, the implication that he had the authority to be the spokesperson for a large, nebulous "community." That his was the only gay voice was problematic.

Class commenced with an overhead listing statements that we were to agree or disagree with as a way of sparking discussion. The beginning of the list focused on gender in schools. At the end of the list, the statements focused on sexuality (e.g., we were asked to agree or disagree with statements such as "You believe you will teach a gay or lesbian student" and "You believe you will have a gay or lesbian colleague"). These statements assumed that everyone in the room was straight. Of 85 M.Ed. students from English, social studies, and foreign language ed, I couldn't have been the only gay one. I waited for the statement directed at LGBTQ educators, but none came. I had never before understood compulsory heterosexuality so clearly as that day when I witnessed and participated in its enactment. Student comments ranged from outrage that sexuality was even an issue we were wasting time on in an education class (e.g., "It goes against everything I believe in," "I don't want to know about people's sex life," "There's no place for homosexuality in my classroom," "I have content to teach") to an admission that, because of a lack of knowledge regarding issues pertinent to LGBT people, fear of saying the wrong thing might prevent teachers from addressing it in their classrooms. Caroline fought a brave fight, with minimal student support, against a vociferous, aggressively hateful student, while I (and any other invisible LGBTQ students in that room) sat, passive, reduced to a hypothetical problem the straight people would have to struggle with in their careers.

I had encountered overt homophobia before, but the insidious current of it that pulsed through this class was more deeply frightening to me—it was hard to tease out. This was a master's-level course at one of the largest universities in the country. If there was no place for me here, there was definitely no place for me in K–12 public schools. I sat in hysterical silence, an accomplice to my own erasure. Later, I imagined how differently class might have gone—and how subsequent classes might go—if there wasn't such thick silence surrounding LGBTQ issues. If I'd found the courage to speak. If my colleagues had been exposed to LGBTQ issues—or people—in school.

I left class wanting to drop out of the program. I emailed Caroline, who convinced me to stay by saying, essentially, that the ignorance that upset me was exactly why schools needed people like me. Quitting equated to a tacit agreement that queer people did not belong in classrooms. Starting the next day, whenever I participated in class I connected the topic of discussion to "my gay experience."

I remembered my own high school experience. Whispered rumors circulated about two women teachers who'd lived together for 20 years, but no one named it out loud. I was suddenly struck by the sheer volume of things we are taught through silence. It now felt like an ethical obligation for me to be out in my classroom, for myself, and for my students, both gay and straight. Our futures would be better if they knew a gay teacher who cared about them, who wasn't predatory, who didn't describe sex acts. It seemed as though, very quickly, the taboo behind the idea would be nullified. I weighed the risks: Students might not respect me; other faculty might shun me; parents might come after me; the administration might not support me. I could lose a job because I created too much controversy or not get hired in the first place since, at the time, our state's equal opportunity employment act did not protect LGBTQ people. But did I really want to teach what I'd learned in school? Did I really want straight students to believe it was their right to silence and marginalize gay people? Did I really want gay students to believe that there was no space for them in the world of grown people?

My Job as a High School English Teacher

In the midst of my job application frenzy, Caroline told me about an urban, arts-based charter high school that was about to open. I made it clear in the interview for a position in that school that I would be out in my classroom. The chief administrator said he was committed to diversity. Currently, the school is in its 6th year of operation; I am in my 6th year of teaching. I have taught at the school since its inception. I have taught all four grade levels, but for the past few years, I've taught 9th- and 10th-grade English. One of my pedagogical goals is to read and write texts with students to challenge the status quo that works to oppress and erase people who deviate from the norm. Because I believe that students learn from all available texts—teacher, other students, course content, and environmental context (the classroom and the sociopolitical atmosphere)—I present myself as an out queer text to disrupt homophobia. To closet myself in my classroom seems to me to reflect a tacit agreement that LGBTQ people should be silent, invisible. Another one of my major pedagogical goals is to cover our state-mandated 10th-grade English language arts standards. The school does not have a required curriculum: I can choose the content I teach as long as I can demonstrate how I am using the content to teach the standards.

Coming Out

I came out to my students the 2nd week of school in my 1st year of teaching. The 9th graders in 5th period were chatty. Not strong readers, not strong writers, but very strong talkers. The 2nd week of school, we were discussing gender roles, and a boy said he felt pressured to dress like a "thug" to avoid being perceived as gay. Tasha commented, "Yeah, Ms. Lauren, I bet all the time people think you're gay because your hair's so short."

"Well, I am gay," I said.

Silence.

"If I'd have known that's all it took to get you to be quiet," I said, "I would've told you a lot sooner."

I told them they could ask me whatever questions they had. What did my parents say? Did I have a girlfriend? How did I know I was gay? The discussion went well. The students shared experiences they'd had with gay people—family members, friends—and with the bullying targeted at people who are perceived as gay. They were attentive and seemed genuinely interested. Some of them were probably thinking hateful things; however, no one said anything hateful. The English teacher had just come out as a lesbian to her class of 9th graders and the world had not come to a crashing halt.

Three weeks later, Kurt suddenly disappeared from fifth period. I asked his cousin where he'd gone. Marc stared at the tops of his shoes. "His mom sent him to his home school."

"Why?"

Silence.

"Marc?"

"She didn't agree with the lifestyle choices of some of the teachers," he said quietly.

I panicked. I was the only teacher who had what could be euphemistically construed as a "lifestyle." I had driven a student away. The principal assured and reassured me that this parent's homophobia was not my fault, or my problem, but I experienced inner conflict. *I can't teach anything if I have no students.* Wasn't it better to teach literacy skills from the closet than to come out and teach to empty desks? Had I made the right decision? My idealism flickered.

The Effects of Being Out at School

I believe I did make the right decision. Since then, the results of my being out have been predominantly positive. I've attended school dances with my partner, and students are always eager to introduce themselves and meet her. Last year, my partner and I had a baby. Students and colleagues alike have been very welcoming of my family. I know my workplace is a welcoming environment for LGBTQ adults, and if I had chosen to closet myself, I would never have known that. I am comfortable at school and feel like a more effective teacher because of it. I connect well with students because I'm not hiding behind fear. For students, it is harder to continue to believe a stereotype when they meet me as an out gay teacher. Although I have no empirical evidence to support this claim, in my teaching career, students tend to engage more with the content when they know hatred is not tolerated in my class, perhaps because they feel less vulnerable to attack, regardless of their sexualities. My students trust and respect me—even those who believe that homosexuality is a sin—because I am honest. That trust creates a culture in which if a student makes a homophobic comment, other students will police them.

My 1st year of teaching, I told students that National Coming Out Day was October 11th. The day celebrates the anniversary of the first March on Washington for lesbian and gay rights. On college campuses, students who support equality for LGBTQ people are supposed to wear jeans and a white T-shirt. More than half the students in each of my classes wore blue jeans and white T-shirts on National Coming Out Day, showing that students felt safe enough at school to publicly express support for LGBTQ people. (The other half wore pajamas, as it was also "Wear Your PJs to School Day.") During my 3rd year of teaching, Aniyah, in her 1st-day-of-school introduction in 10th grade, said, "You know, Lauren, when I first came up in this school last year, I heard it was all kinds of gay people, and I swore if any of them came up to me, I would pop 'em in their mouth. But now, it's cool. The other day my mom and cousin were talking stuff about gay people and I told them, 'Shut up. It ain't all like that. Y'all don't even know what y'all are talking about.'" Her comment illustrates that knowing a gay person can lead students to reassess—and potentially to change—homophobic views. When students demonstrate their support in these explicit ways, LGBTQ students can feel safer at school knowing they have allies. And when students feel safer, they are more likely to continue attending school, thus increasing the likelihood of their academic success.

Gay-Straight Alliance. We finally started a gay-straight alliance in my 5th year of teaching. The GSA gives students another signal that the school strives to be inclusive and gives students space to openly discuss their relationships, experiences with homophobia, and strategies for making positive change. They took their efforts to make positive change to the statehouse in the middle of the school year. Three students lobbied the education committee for an antibullying bill. Each student wrote his or her own testimony advocating that LGBTQ students be specifically enumerated as protected by this bill. They were the only students there—all the other lobbyists were adults—yet they maintained their poise.

During the 2007–2008 school year in the GSA, transgender issues came to the fore for me. I have a friend who is trans, and from him, I learned how much work needs to be done to promote equality for trans people—a point made exceedingly obvious by the fight in the Senate to take transgender people out of the protection of the Employment Non-Discrimination Act in order that it may pass to protect gay people in the workplace. I did two different activities this year to start promoting trans awareness at school. First, in GSA, I showed *Ma Vie en Rose* (Berliner, 1997), the story of a 6-year-old in France who identifies as a girl but was born male. Later in the year, GSA brought in a panel from TransOhio, the local transgender advocacy group, to talk to 10th graders about what it's like to be trans and the issues trans people face, especially at work, in families, and dating. Students were very receptive to the panel and asked questions throughout. In the class discussion following the panel, students compared what the panelists said to things they had seen on the recent *Oprah* episode about transgender youth.

Book Group. Students also participated in the book group organized by the Pink TIGers. We read young adult novels that contained gay and lesbian characters and addressed LGBTQ issues, such as *Boy Meets Boy* (Levithan, 2003) and *The Perks of Being a Wallflower* (Chbosky, 1999), then met with students from other area high schools at a queer youth center to discuss the books. We did not read any LGBTQ-specific novels in English class, and this gave students access to books they might not have been able to get otherwise and a welcoming space outside school to meet queer and ally youth. The students who participated this year loved the book group discussions and were always eager to get the next book and meet again.

However, the first of the book club meetings ended in the most frightening experience I've had being an out teacher. Crystal, a 9th-grade student, had expressed excitement about the book group. She had finished the book *The Perks of Being a Wallflower* by Stephen Chbosky (1999), in 2 days and passed it along to another student. The day before the book club meeting, she approached me and said, "I'm sorry about what my dad is going to do to you."

"What is your dad going to do to me?" I asked calmly, as if calmness might dismantle this implied threat. She told me he refused to allow her to participate in the book group. Her dad had kicked her 16-year-old brother out of the house when he came out as gay because her father didn't want any gays around his kids. She also told me that she intended to sneak onto a different bus after school and come to the meeting anyway. I recommended she not defy her father.

Before the book club meeting, I mentioned that conversation to Mollie (author of Chapter 10) because it had worried me. If he had kicked his own son out and would "do something" to me, the gay teacher, what damage might he do to his daughter? Crystal did show up at the youth center that afternoon. She said she'd wanted to come because she was gay, but her dad wasn't open to gay stuff, and told us how he had kicked her brother out of the house. She participated in the discussion about the book and seemed to enjoy herself.

After the discussion, the youth left. I heard a man coming up the stairs demanding to find his daughter. A volunteer was on his heels asking who his daughter was. He arrived at the top of the stairs and said her name. He'd never met me before, and I didn't want this to be our first introduction. He was very large and obviously furious. I shook my head at the volunteer, and he told the dad that his daughter might have left. The dad looked around, then went out front and shouted about what he was going to do to his daughter and that gay teacher who brought her to this place.

What was he going to do to Crystal? To me? I called my two school administrators to let them know what had happened. The next morning at school, I told every adult in my hall and the office what had happened and described the man's features in case he showed up. The front doors were locked, so at least he would have to ring the bell and be let in before coming to get me.

Crystal and her dad got to school around 10 o'clock. The assistant administrator came down to my room to tell me I was needed in a meeting in the principal's office. I met with Crystal, her dad, and the principal. The principal introduced me as the English teacher and asked me, "You don't teach any classes in being gay, do you, Ms. Lauren?" The dad started ranting. "Crystal didn't come home from the bus last night, so after about an hour, I got worried and called the police. I didn't know this event was happening last night. When my wife got home, she told me that's where Crystal had probably gone, so I went there to get her. I had told her not to go, and she snuck on the wrong bus and walked down to that place. This school promotes gayness, and I was suspicious; you're a gay teacher, and you gave my daughter a gay book and then invited her to the gay establishment—and I went in there, I walked up those stairs, I saw all those freaks; I know what kind of place that is and what you're trying to do, filling her head with all this stuff about straight people don't understand us. She's a vulnerable 14-year-old. She didn't have my permission to be there. Why didn't I get a phone call?"

When I offered explanations or clarification, he ignored me. The principal repeated that this school was safe for all students, even those who might have different values, and kept trying to revert his focus from my sexuality to Crystal and her disobedience.

He withdrew her from the school. The first time a parent had withdrawn a student using my sexuality as a reason, I doubted myself. This time, I had had 4 years of active work against homophobia and heterosexism in school behind me. As frightening and difficult as the incident was for me, I knew I was doing this work because I wanted to prevent my students from developing (or maintaining) hateful attitudes like his. My first concern was for Crystal. I worried about what other consequences there were for her. Could she protect herself? He had invaded two spaces in which I felt safe. I felt violated, and I'm an adult who never has to see him again. I feel lucky that the school is a safe space and the principal is supportive. I wish that didn't have to feel like luck.

A parent had accused me of trying to make his daughter gay. My biggest fear had been realized. And it didn't stop me from continuing to work against hatred; it didn't stop me from being out at school. I wonder if Crystal's dad and people like him would be less hateful had they had out gay teachers or read queer-inclusive texts in school.

Reading Queer-Inclusive Texts

Susan Talburt (2000) writes about "Olivia," a lesbian university professor who resists students' attempts to read her as a text by not coming out in her graduate classes. She seeks to diminish her textual presence to focus attention on the print texts for the course (see entry in the Annotated Bibliography of this book). When students walk into my classroom, they "read" me as a text. As I stand before them, a young, White, middle-class woman, they "read" me. When I select print texts for class, they "read" me. Instead of trying to deny my textual presence, I choose to assert it in a particular way. However, as I select print texts for class, I feel torn between the desire to read queer-inclusive literature as a way to promote equity, and the fear of what Olivia articulates: If we read *any* queer-inclusive literature, students will dismiss me as the gay teacher who teaches *only* gay stuff. Their parents may accuse me of trying to make them gay. Students complain that an African American teacher who teaches American history only teaches about the civil rights movement, and a Jewish teacher—who teaches the same American history curriculum—only teaches about the Holocaust. Yet neither of these teachers relies solely on her ethnicity to promote equity. How can I expect the mere fact of my sexuality to promote equity? Being out has not prevented homophobic outbursts. For example, in my 1st year of teaching, one boy punched another in the mouth and called him a "fucking faggot" because he claimed the boy had "propositioned" him. The boy denied the allegation. (A sort of reversal of that incident happened the next year. A student punched another in the face for making a homophobic comment.) Just this year, a student was expelled for verbally antagonizing an out gay boy at school. At first, the gay student denied it was happening because he feared what the bully might do. I realized that I needed to do more that just "be out" to fight homophobia in my school. My reasons for avoiding gay texts in my classroom were admittedly about protecting myself, not about offering students rich and diverse reading experiences, or about promoting social justice.

Joining this teacher inquiry group impelled me to think more critically about my textual presence in my classroom. While many queer students feel safe being out at school, most of the out queer students are White. Many Black students identify as gay or bisexual to some teachers, and to other Black students on the down low, but they closet themselves in the context of the school at large. More than one Black student has commented that being gay is a "White thing." Comments like this one, and the fact that so few Black students feel safe enough to come out at school, forced me to question whether my being out challenges students' homophobia in the way I believe it does. I can only be one example of a gay person, and if I want my students to expand their concepts of what's possible for them, I don't want to be the only template they have for "gay." How does being an out queer text in my classroom limit certain possibilities, as it opens others, and for whom? How does reading queer-inclusive literature affect students' attitudes about LGBTQ people and the issues that affect them?

I finally felt empowered to start using queer-inclusive texts in my classroom after the theater department staged *The Laramie Project* (Kaufman, 2001) with our students in the fall of 2004, during the presidential election, in the midst of the fierce debate over lesbian and gay marriage rights. *The*

Laramie Project is a play about Matthew Shepard, a gay man who was kidnapped, beaten, tied to a fence, and left to die in Laramie, Wyoming. After the production, the students who performed and those who watched seemed to understand gay rights issues in more complex and immediate ways than they had just knowing a few gay people. They identified with the characters. I want them to meet more queer characters in texts. Using LGBTQ-inclusive literature and film erodes the silence—these characters, their lives and experiences, deserve textual and discursive space in the classroom. They are worth being written about; they are worth being read about. The support of the teachers in this inquiry group helped me to surmount my own fears and introduce LGBTQ texts in my class.

Splashing Around, or, A Few Early Efforts

As an out lesbian, teaching queer-inclusive texts felt dangerous to me. I feared parents, like Kurt's mom, withdrawing their children from the school, and, like Crystal's dad, accusing me of "converting" their children to the gay "lifestyle." Even so, in my first 3 years of teaching, I did use some LGBTQ texts. My 1st year teaching, we read the Disposable Heroes of Hiphoprisy's rap/poem "Language of Violence" (Franti, 1992) together. The ensuing discussion was messy—I don't remember the details—but everything was messy my 1st year of teaching, so it didn't seem unique to the topic.

My 2nd year of teaching, I allowed students a lot of latitude in choosing young adult novels. I gave them lists of suggestions, and two of the suggested texts had queer main characters: *Rainbow Boys*, by Alex Sanchez (2003), and *Annie on My Mind*, by Nancy Garden (2007/1982). Some of the other selections included gay characters, such as *True Believer*, by Virginia Euwer Wolff (2003), and *Weetzie Bat*, by Francesca Lia Block (2004). Students completed individual projects on these texts, but we did not engage them as a whole class.

When I joined this inquiry group at the beginning of my 3rd year of teaching, I was seeking both strategies for incorporating queer-inclusive texts and support as issues, if any, arose.

During one inquiry group meeting, we discussed secretary of education Margaret Spellings's threat to revoke government funding if the Public Broadcasting System aired the Sugartime! episode of *Postcards from Buster* (Gunther, 2005) (see entry in the Annotated Bibliography of this book). In general, the show is about a cartoon rabbit who goes to different places, meets different people, and produces documentaries about culture. In this particular episode, Buster visits kids in Vermont who have two moms and learns to make maple syrup and cheese. We were preparing for the state-mandated graduation test in my 10th-grade classes. To incorporate a queer-inclusive text while continuing to teach state standards, I brought in a *Washington Post* article about the debate. We read the article together, aloud, and discussed author bias, then they invented graduation test–style questions about the article. When they were finished, we discussed their views on the topic, then they wrote brief responses. During the discussion, I asked questions such as "When did you first know what the word 'gay' meant?" "Did it have a positive or negative connotation?" "Do you think you should be protected from learning about certain issues as young adults?" In their written responses, one student said that maybe really young kids shouldn't be exposed to "that" because they might not understand it. Another said he thought Spellings was a "dumb-ass." Overall, the responses were supportive of the families in the *Buster* episode. I don't know how many of them were just writing what they thought I wanted them to write, of course, but they were thinking about the issue.

It's important to read texts dealing with issues affecting students. Adolescents are trying to figure out who they are and what they believe. They connect with identity issues, like sexuality. They are interested in their worlds, and sexuality is, in the United States and elsewhere, politically contentious. When students relate to a topic, they see intrinsic value in it. Reading about diverse characters not only helps diverse students find themselves in literature, it also helps all students develop empathy for others, including people very different from them. In addition, they more willingly read and discuss, developing literacy skills.

Diving In, or, Really Giving It a Try

It was the 3rd week of the 2005–2006 school year, and I was already out to my students. I decided to try to determine whether reading queer-inclusive texts made a difference in student attitudes. To kick off this study, I started class with a prereading questionnaire[2] to find out what attitudes students bring with them to school. Next, we read "A Letter to Harvey Milk" (Newman, 1988) (see entry in the Annotated Bibliography of this book). Then we had a brief, open-ended discussion. After the discussion, they wrote a 200-word response to the story. The prompt was open-ended; they could write anything about the story. The final part of the study was an anonymous, voluntary questionnaire, on which I asked five questions.

I also had to cover the state's English language arts standards in order to prepare students to take the state-mandated graduation test and to be able to defend my choice of text to concerned parents. Each year, the first unit I do in my 10th-grade classes is about personal narrative. We cover elements of narrative such as point of view, setting, conflict, and character, all of which are state standards, while at the same time discussing the issues raised in the texts. Students complete daily writing exercises designed to help them practice concepts as they work toward a complete draft of their personal narratives.

Most of the essays we read are from *Starting with "I": Personal Essays by Teenagers* (Estepa, 1997). Topics run the gamut from difficult issues, such as gang violence and ethnic profiling, to lighter issues, such as music and shopping with Mom. We also read narratives from established authors and celebrities. The texts I choose for this unit are generally nonfiction, but I introduce first-person fictional narratives as well. One such fictional narrative we read was Lesléa Newman's (1988) short story "A Letter to Harvey Milk," which I mentioned previously. It's a compelling story set in San Francisco in 1985, narrated by Harry, an elderly Jewish man. He is a Holocaust survivor taking a writing class at the senior center. Several gay characters appear in the story. It is the reading of this text and the surrounding events that I examine next.

Prereading Questionnaire

On the prereading questionnaire, after I came out to them, but before we read the story, several students expressed ambivalence in the form of apathy or moral relativism when describing their attitudes about homosexuality, for example, "I really don't care 'cause I know I like boys" to "I don't care about it, as long as they don't try to hit on me" to "To me homosexuality is wrong . . . God says in the Bible . . . but I accept people who have chosen to be homosexual." Beneath these answers and others like them, I read them grappling with the issue. They say, in various ways, that they don't care, as long as it has no impact on them, which indicates their belief that there is something wrong with it, and they do not want to be implicated in it.

Only one student claimed not to know any gay people, and only one student identified as bi-curious. With the exception of one, all the respondents said they'd seen gay characters on TV or in movies. Many cited parents, friends, and church as influences on their beliefs about homosexuality. Suddenly, they were being asked—on a questionnaire given by an out lesbian authority figure—to interrogate and articulate their beliefs. Because they were writing for my class, because they knew they were supposed to accept people, they hesitated to express overt homophobia, even if it was their actual position.

This same ambivalence comes through in their responses to how they would react if they were mistaken for the opposite sexuality. One student writes: "I would be angry/pissed off because I know I'm not. On the other hand I wouldn't be angry because I know I'm not." Another student writes, "I would not be offended, but I would be uncomfortable." It's difficult to accurately assess attitudes they bring with them to school from a questionnaire they have to respond to in class. However, I believe that their ambivalence demonstrates that they are engaging with the issue. Ambivalence wants to be resolved, whether that resolution comes by refusing to think about something, or by finding more information to help clarify the issue. Because ambivalence often results from not knowing, introducing queer-inclusive texts when they are in a state of unknowing gives them the information their ambivalent minds crave. It makes refusing to think about it a lot more difficult.

Reading and Responding to "A Letter to Harvey Milk"

As we read the description of physical intimacy between two men in a concentration camp, at least one student in each class laughed or expressed disgust. In one postreading class discussion, I asked if they liked the story. One student said, "It was sad and nasty." I asked why. He responded, "They shouldn't have killed him, but it was too much description." I asked if it would have been too much had the description been of a man and a woman. The student said, "That's different." When I asked how, he said, "It just is." He went on to say, "My dad would punch me in my chest until I couldn't breathe if I was gay. . . . Because I'm his only son." I asked him if he thought he should be allowed to be anything he wanted and he laughed. "I don't want to be that," he said. "It's nasty." That he was voicing a position before the entire class—and me—obviously tempered his response. Whether he asserted his homophobia more strongly to protect himself from the possible homophobia of his peers or less strongly because he didn't want me to penalize him, I don't know.

Out of all the classes that read the story, his comment was the most negative. In other discussions, students wondered whether Izzie was "really" gay or whether Harry might be gay for letting Izzie sleep in bed with him. They were surprised that the Nazis imprisoned gay and lesbian people and shocked at the violence of the beating and shooting of Yussl. They asked questions about Harvey Milk's life, shocked that he, too, had been murdered because he was gay. Two students said they wished the story had given them more information about Harvey Milk.

Their questions and comments demonstrate that classrooms are legitimate spaces for reading and discussing queer-inclusive texts. Students engaged with the story. They empathized with the characters—even the student who said, "It's nasty" also said it was sad. When students empathize with characters, in this case, gay characters, they can't easily objectify them. The negative stereotypes that lead to homophobia begin to break down.

Postreading Questionnaire

In the end-of-semester questionnaire, after having read *Biloxi Blues* (Simon, 1998)—a play about a young man who meets a wide range of people, including a gay man, when he is drafted into the United States Army during World War II and sent to Biloxi, Mississippi, for basic training—and "A Letter to Harvey Milk," (Newman, 1988) and after they had a debate in history class about gay marriage, three students claimed not to have encountered any queer-inclusive print or visual text in any classes. I'm not sure what to make of that. They could be so uncomfortable with the topic that they are trying to distance themselves from LGBT content, or they could think reading texts with LGBTQ characters is so unremarkable that they don't even remember it, because it wasn't a big deal. What I take from these three responses is that it's important to integrate queer-inclusive texts across the year, not just in one unit. Exposing students to queer characters and issues over time avoids the foods-and-festivals pitfall (Banks, 1997). It also makes it more difficult for students to dismiss having read them. Their opinions about reading texts with LGBTQ characters in school reflected their understanding that they are supposed to be open-minded: "It can open people's mind to things they had never thought of before." Students tended to be much more specific in their answer to the question about having LGBTQ teachers. One student wrote: "One of my favorite teachers is gay. We still have fun in her class and get lots of homework." Another says: "I love my LGBTQ teacher." There was an interesting split in these answers. Some students said having an LGBTQ teacher was no different from having a straight teacher, implying that we're all the same, or that they just don't see difference. Some students, on the other hand, wrote that they liked it because they got to hear different points of view, or because "most schools I have . . . attended do not . . . hire LGBTQ teachers and having one tells me this school is a safe and accepting school, the kind I have been looking for for a very long time." These comments lead me to believe that being out as a teacher helps some students feel safer, but because it is singular, it does little to push students to recognize the wider problems of homophobia and heterosexism.

Most of the students claimed not to have changed their opinions about LGBTQ people and wrote that they didn't care what other people do or are. They don't mind reading about LGBTQ people and issues in school; it makes no difference if they have LGBTQ teachers. The major exception was a student who, in the earlier questionnaire, wrote that gay people "make her skin crawl." In the February questionnaire, she admits to a complete change of heart when she says she has "more respect for them now, especially since I discovered my sister is a lesbian. They are the sweetest people." While this answer initially made me think that knowing gay people is most effective at reducing students' homophobia, I also recognize that her answer is just as reductive as "They make my skin crawl." Such a broad generalization renders it meaningless. Part of the problem is the dichotomy I created by framing the question the way I did. However, they express less discomfort with the issues on the end-of-semester questionnaire, which indicates to me that reading about and discussing LGBTQ issues and characters alleviated some of the ambivalence they expressed on the first questionnaire. Acquiring information from reading and discussing queer-inclusive texts—being proactive as opposed to reactive—might have undermined rather than caused an uproar.

Reflections

These 10th-grade students took the graduation test in March 2006. Ninety-eight percent of students passed the reading portion, and 87% passed the writing portion. A lot of factors contribute to their success on the test—small class size, among other things—but based on my experience, reading texts that get students to engage with LGBTQ issues does not negatively affect their ability to perform above average on the state standardized test. And getting students to grapple with difficult issues—reading about them, writing about them, talking about them—helps them learn to question their assumptions and to challenge the status quo.

Talburt's (2000) "Olivia" discusses her belief that coming out actually reifies homophobia by creating a false dichotomy between LGBTQ people and others. In turn, when a student is asked on a questionnaire to state his or her opinion about LGBTQ people, he or she is forced either to qualify what he or she says, or to generalize in an absurd way, as in "They are the sweetest people!" Instead of creating a space for ongoing dialogue, I oversimplified a complex issue. Even so, the students who contradict themselves, who grapple with the issue, demonstrate their attempts to negotiate the complexity of the issues and contextual politics. Reading queer-inclusive texts raises questions they may never have encountered before. And answering those questions for themselves matters. That's learning: using information they've read to reflect on what they believe and why, learning to express their views and listen to others'. When students connect what they read to their own lives, they are employing comprehension strategies that will help them to succeed on high-stakes tests, and throughout the rest of their lives.

I believe that, as a lesbian, coming out at school has helped fight homophobia, not reify it, by allowing me to be honestly myself. Students ask a lot of questions, and dodging them seems to generate even more interest in what's not being said. But the fact of being out is not the end of the fight. Engaging the issue using varied texts, rather than avoiding it, allows them to confront their fears—a great reason to continue reading queer-inclusive texts and to continue being out. Current sociopolitical forces work to keep LGBTQ people in the closet; thus, creating space is necessary: space in my classroom, and, I hope, space in my students, for the empathy that incites social action.

Notes

1. This heading is a play on the song lyric used by Pink: "I'm comin' up, so you better get this party started" (Perry, 2001).

2. The questionnaire contained five questions: (1) What are your beliefs about homosexuality? (2) Who or what has influenced those beliefs? (3) Do you know any LGBTQ people? (4) Have you read any books or seen any TV shows or movies containing LGBTQ characters? and (5) If you are straight, how would you react if someone mistook you for gay? If you are gay or bisexual, how would you react if someone mistook you for straight?

References

Banks, J. A. (1997). Approaches to cultural curriculum reform. In J. A. Banks & C. A. M. Banks (Eds.), *Multicultural education: Issues and perspectives* (pp. 229–250). Boston: Allyn & Bacon.

Berliner, A. (Director). (1997). *Ma vie en rose* [Motion picture]. France: Sony Picture Classics.

Block, F. L. (2004). *Weetzie Bat.* New York: HarperCollins.

Chbosky, S. (1999). *The perks of being a wallflower.* New York: MTV Books.

Estepa, A. (Ed.). (1997). *Starting with "I": Personal essays by teenagers.* New York: Persea Books.

Franti, M. (1992). Language of violence [The Disposable Heroes of Hiphoprisy]. On *Hypocrisy is the greatest luxury* [CD]. New York: 4th & B'way/Island/Poly Gram Records.

Garden, N. (2007/1982). *Annie on my mind.* New York: Farrar, Strauss & Giroux.

Gunther, J. (Director). (2005, March 22). *Postcards from Buster:* "Sugartime!" [Television broadcast]. Columbus, OH: Public Broadcasting Service.

Kaufman, M. (2001). *The Laramie project.* New York: Vintage.

Levithan, D. (2003). *Boy meets boy.* New York: Alfred A. Knopf.

Newman, L. (1988). A letter to Harvey Milk. *A letter to Harvey Milk: Short stories* (pp. 25–28). Ithaca, NY: Firebrand Books.

Perry, L. (2001). Get the party started. [Recorded by Pink]. On *Missundazstood.* [CD]. New York: La Face.

Sanchez, A. (2003). *Rainbow boys.* New York: Simon Pulse.

Simon, N. (1998). Biloxi blues. *The collected plays of Neil Simon* (Vol. 4). New York: Simon & Schuster.

Talburt, S. (2000). On not coming out, or, Reimagining limits. In W. J. Spurlin (Ed.), *Lesbian and gay studies and the teaching of English: Positions, pedagogies, and cultural politics* (pp. 54–78). Urbana, IL: National Council of Teachers of English.

Wolff, V. E. (2003). *True believer.* London: Faber Children's Books.

5

Risk and Threat
in Critical Inquiry
Vacancies, Violations, and Vacuums

JASON GONZALES

T HIS CHAPTER IS AN EXPLORATION of my efforts to be an ally as a high school English teacher and sponsor of a gay-straight alliance (GSA). In it, I reflect on the risks I took and the threat I experienced and consider the supports that need to be in place in order to challenge students to engage in similar kinds of work.

Vacancy: As in, My Job, or, "So, You Want to Get Fired, Eh?"

I was standing at the photocopier in late September, about 3 weeks into the school year, when a teacher noticed a copy of the short story "A Letter to Harvey Milk," by Lesléa Newman (1988), in my hand (see entry in the Annotated Bibliography of this book). After seeing the title, he said, "So . . . you want to get fired, eh?"

I assumed that the teacher's reaction was not because he had ever read the story or was even necessarily familiar with the author, who has written other LGBTQ-themed stories, including picture books. I presumed that it was merely seeing Harvey Milk's name and recognizing him as a gay politician and activist. Even at the time, though, I recognized that this was a complex moment that I could not quickly extract all the possible meanings from. Instead, it just made me anxious and sweaty. I was in my 1st year of employment in the district. My gut reaction was to take this as a wake-up call. Here was a veteran teacher who had previously presented himself as friendly, helpful, and not particularly interested in maintaining the status quo through his teaching. But at that moment, he said something that presented an indirect threat, by voicing the threat as if it were a force *out there* that I would be unleashing on myself. I understood his message to be, "I won't endanger your job, but if you have students read this, someone might." And, in fact, when I would talk about using this and other texts that had LGBTQ content, teachers would say things like "I'm glad *you're* taking it on." The omission in their statement is that they were not willing to take on discussions of sexuality, despite sensing the need for it.

Understanding Threat as a Site for Critical Inquiry

In this chapter I look at moments like these from my 1st year of being a secondary English teacher and an ally. Specifically, I think through moments when I sensed threat as moments when questioning stops or is likely to stop because of that sensation. I single out these moments for their potential to learn something about how and why sexuality should be a site for critical inquiry. Throughout this essay I will use the term *threat* as Fecho (2001) does:

> It is my belief that a critical inquiry classroom, when it is functioning well, teeters on the fulcrum of threat. There is no avoiding it. The nature of the work coupled to the prior experiences of all stakeholders creates varying degrees of threat within all individually and collectively. I could call this feeling discomfort or some other term that is less provocative. But to do so is to devalue the importance of the emotion and therefore relegate it to some educational backburner. For me discomfort is what someone feels when wearing a sweater on a day that turns too warm or that pins and needles feeling in a driver's leg after being too long behind the wheel. However, when teachers shy away from controversy in the classroom, parents ask for changes in their children's curriculum, or students construct a new sense of their worldview, some aspect of their lives has come under some degree of threat. (p. 30)

I can identify two kinds of impediments that were in the forefront as I attempted to be an ally teacher, that is, a teacher working as an advocate for LGBTQ people. There were threats (real and imagined) from authority, but another impediment was not having a construct for how to plan effectively for and react to the literacy events that presented a threat to my students. In this chapter I try to understand better these events in which reading or writing plays a central role in two ways. One way is to analyze my experience when I felt a sense of threat, which often happened at the same time as when the students felt a sense of threat. Another is to imagine a reshaping of each literacy event in such a way that students might gain some insight into where their feelings might come from.

The difficulty of telling my story lies in representing myself as I was in the moment of each vignette versus my way of thinking over a year later. To help with this, I attempt to recount each vignette as true to how I thought at the time and follow each with a reflection that represents my current understandings.

Critical inquiry is a useful, focused way to imagine and analyze. But because I am analyzing my own narrative, my evidence comes from anecdotal observations and my own thoughts and feelings. Luckily, there is an important reason to consider my thoughts and feelings, for certainly there are a number of teachers out there who find themselves in situations similar to mine. I want to make one thing clear: I have been an activist teacher, but in the name of keeping order in the classroom, one peril that I may have fallen prey to is using constructs of teaching and learning that reproduce oppressive models. The truth is, they are really hard to escape. As the teacher, I had a certain degree of authority; both privileges and responsibilities came with this authority, privileges and responsibilities that students lacked. Such is the status quo of the classroom. The status quo is hard to change, and it is not easy to enact sudden changes (or at least not without repercussions). And this chapter is a thinking-through of what it meant to attempt to challenge it, while at times still obviously working within it.

The High School

My first full-time English position was in 2005 at this high school, where I taught for a 1½ years before getting laid off because of reductions in staff. It is an urban, alternative high school for the arts. Because it is an alternative high school, students enroll there through a lottery process. While many students enter the lottery to take advantage of the college preparatory academics and arts-centered curriculum, others enter to avoid what they perceive to be rough neighborhood high schools. The school is also perceived to be a safe place for LGBTQ teens, whether they choose to be out or not. Perhaps the school is perceived this way because of its focus on the arts and the stereotype of gay people being artistic. Perhaps it is because artistic people are sometimes thought to be more accepting of diversity. These reasons deserve more careful scrutiny and inquiry that I won't get into here. For now, I think it is sufficient to say that having a school where gay teens can feel a sense of refuge from the places where they perceive threat is beneficial.

Once I was at the high school, I had a growing awareness of the need to address homophobia and heterosexism, despite its reputation as a safe place for LGBTQ teens. My understanding of *how* to address these domains was unformed. By this time, though, I had joined the Pink TIGers and could get support from them.

Violations:
Reading "A Letter to Harvey Milk" with 9th Graders

The story "A Letter to Harvey Milk" (Newman, 1988) is told from the point of view of an elderly concentration camp survivor who is taking a writing course from a young Jewish lesbian. One of the things he writes is a letter to the deceased Harvey Milk, who was the first openly gay city supervisor of San Francisco. A critical part of the story is when the narrator relates a story from a friend who was in the Nazi concentration camps. The friend tells him about how he and a male friend would comfort each other in the camp by sleeping together. The teller uses vague and nonexplicit language, saying only that they would "touch each other" (p. 28). The story ends with his friend's public murder at the hands of Nazi guards. We read the story aloud in my 9th-grade classes after the encounter at the copier. As we read, a steady stream of sweat ran down the center of my back. At the mention of the two men in a concentration camp holding each other, the class became unnaturally quiet. Sounds of clothes rustling and throats clearing that would normally be unnoticeable stood out.

Even though the students were visibly uncomfortable and my autonomic fear responses were kicking in (no thanks to the teacher at the copier), I believed that stories like this *needed* to be read. None of the readings I had used before offered similar opportunities to inquire into homophobia and heteronormativity. Furthermore, I thought it advantageous that this story foregrounded gay and lesbian characters in ways that made it easier for students to sympathize with them. I felt a mix of determination and fear during and after this first reading in class. I made certain that I collected all copies of the story as the bell rang—and not just to save paper. As the students filed out, a girl who had previously come out to me as bisexual asked, "Won't you get fired for having us read this?" She still looked quite anxious after I replied, "Don't worry. It's fine."

In reflecting on this vignette, I now understand it this way: The need I felt for reading this story was a need for critical inquiry. What I called *discomfort* at the time, I would now characterize as *threat*. The girl in the vignette gave voice to a direct threat. The threat was to normative behavior in the English classroom: Certain kinds of sexual identities are expected to be represented in classroom texts. I included this story in a unit on the theme of courage, and approaching the story using critical inquiry within this context was difficult for me.

I asked students to come up with discussion questions about the story. Admittedly, this was a bit of a dodge on my part. Sensing threat, I assumed that allowing them to come up with discussion questions would ensure that they didn't see an *agenda* on my part to the follow-up discussion. I had been teaching the students how to write good discussion questions, and among the most promising questions students asked, with regard to critical inquiry, were ones that asked about characters' feelings and thoughts in reaction to the treatment of the gay and lesbian characters in the story. While this line of questioning had the benefit of asking students to empathize with the characters and perhaps even account for their feelings and reactions, it did nothing to encourage the students to investigate where their ideologies about sexuality come from. In fact, it quite likely positioned students to feel pity for the lesbian and gay characters, a stance that can be counterproductive to queering the power relationships with regard to gender and sex identity. Winans (2006), makes a similar point:

> The goal of this work is not specifically to combat homophobia, for, as scholars such as Deborah P. Britzman (1995) and David Wallace (2002) have argued, such an individually focused, psychological approach can often ignore power, center heterosexuality, and construct a situation in which benevolent heterosexuals are encouraged to tolerate the "sexual other" (Wallace 2002: 153). (pp. 106–107)

Along these lines, I could have asked students to think and write about their own reactions to the story and to account for their reactions, that is, ask them to name the places that their ideas had come from, which would certainly have required some advance teaching. Had I done that, though, would the 9th graders' sense of threat have been heightened to the point of their lashing out at me? Would the threat toward *me* have increased? I was already taking a risk in sharing this story. I had deliberately planned on reading it in class only and keeping all the copies. And my sense of threat was heightened by the comments made by the teacher at the copier. But a class that had already learned something about how to account for where their ideas come from might arguably be better equipped to handle threat. Furthermore, it might have helped go beyond what Winans refers to in the quote above: encouraging "benevolent heterosexuals" to tolerate the "sexual other." While teaching students to be tolerant is not inherently bad, it is a significantly lesser goal than the transformations I aspire to.

In this light, it was perhaps unfair of me not to address, through some kind of preparatory lesson, how this story might have placed my students, whether straight or LGBTQ, in a position of feeling threatened. Arguably, asking them to come up with discussion questions only made them more vulnerable, which alone is not a bad thing, necessarily, but requires instructional support.

One problem here is the confining idea of the traditional lesson. Most high school students are well trained to be on the receiving end of what Paolo Freire (1970) calls the banking model of learning. Freire's model describes the common dynamic in which teachers act as depositors of knowledge that students are expected to passively receive. In keeping with this dominant mode of pedagogy, most students expect to learn something from the story, perhaps with the aid of some discussion. So I can imagine that quite a few of my students expected that I wanted them to learn something like "Nazis are bad guys who killed all kinds of people, including gays."

But by contrast, as a critical inquirer, I want to understand what makes the story possible and what makes the readers' reactions to it possible. What prevented me from doing this was a very powerful sense of threat to *my* goals for introducing the story. For me to pose to 9th graders the question, "How are you feeling about such and such in the story?" would have been an invitation to have them tell me what they thought I wanted to hear, which for the students brave enough to speak at the time would likely have been some version of sympathy or pity for the murdered gay characters. As Winans warns in the quotation above, this ignores power relations and gives the students the opportunity to either be or appear to be tolerant. I struggled to think of a way to follow up a reading of this sort with discussion questions that decenter heterosexuality. However, there are models that I now know of from Mellor, O'Neill, and Patterson (2000) that would be interesting to try. I am thinking specifically of lessons they introduce where students are asked to change the sex of a character, describe how this changes the story, and then account for how they produce these changes. A move into this kind of reading instruction has the benefit of feeling like role-playing, which most students enjoy, but it also encourages a transformational kind of deep understanding by getting into the socially constructed knowledge that is key to new literacies.

Gay-Straight Alliance: What Happens in a Power Vacuum

I facilitated the gay-straight alliance (GSA) and had high hopes for doing some antihomophobia activism alongside student participants. But there were challenges. Throughout the year, meetings were sporadic because of schedule conflicts. Students showed up sporadically as well. One day I would be ready with an article to discuss and two kids would show up. Another day I would need time to grade and more than a dozen students would show up. They were always happy to just hang out and talk about, for example, *American Idol* or *Brokeback Mountain* (Lee, Proulx, & McMurtry, 2005) (see entry in the Annotated Bibliography of this book). I was happy to make a friendly, nonthreatening place for students to get together, but many students and I agreed that the GSA should be involved in some kind of activism. One of my responses to this was to show a documentary called *It's Elementary* (Cohen & Chasnoff, 1996) to watch with the GSA over two consecutive weekly meetings. The film shows several classroom discussions—from elementary school through middle school—where gay and lesbian issues are the subject (see entry in the Annotated Bibliography of this book). After we finished viewing the film we were only able to have very brief discussions about it. Even so, I got a sense of what an impact the film had made. One girl said, "I didn't know you could talk about this stuff in school." We talked about how powerful it would be if we could have such productive discussions in our classrooms at our school.

In many ways the GSA felt ineffective with regard to the pursuit of my goals as an ally. It felt too self-contained. It seemed as though any exploratory talk about sexuality couldn't extend beyond my four walls. Was this work worth doing? What could we have done better? Or was there another way to conceive of the GSA other than as an activist group? For example, I remember Mollie Blackburn (author of Chapter 10) saying that the conversations there could be safe ways to explore and rehearse ways of talking about LGBTQ identities so that students could do more activist work beyond the GSA. I can only hope that was what was going on there.

I discuss my frustration with the GSA not to reveal that GSAs aren't useful or important, but instead to reflect my understanding of their role in my desire to create change. I won't discuss the role of GSAs deeply here except to say that their role in change is valuable but different from the role of engaging a whole class in the kinds of inquiry I outline throughout this chapter. Winans (2006) points out, "Queer pedagogy challenges all students regardless of their sexual identities because it calls into question the process of normalizing dominant assumptions and beliefs, as it challenges instructors to question and to continue to test their own pedagogy" (p. 106). The GSA might have been an apt place for this kind of work, where the student members and I could have engaged in some coinquiry revolving around sexual identities, perhaps through sharing stories or documenting and inquiring about the thoughts and actions of others at the school.

Policing Language and Knowledge Vacuums

My earliest attempts to act as an ally at the high school were reactions to what I saw around me. Some of that included intervening and pointing out hate speech. Early in the year I staked out what wasn't acceptable in my class. When the first unfortunate students uttered the phrase "That's so gay," I leapt on them. I used a rational tone and explained why that kind of speech violates classroom rules. Most kids shook their heads and grimaced with annoyance, as if I didn't get how innocuous this phrase was or how it was okay to think that gayness was equal to weakness, weirdness, and wrongness. I continued to be firm every time something like this came up. My explanation was brief: All students must feel safe and welcome in my classroom and at the school. I also got the sense from the students that I was the only teacher explicitly enforcing this kind of rule.

I interpret the students' reaction to my prohibition against homophobic language as stemming from a threat to the norms of language as they understand them. As a result, I conclude that I missed opportunities by not asking students to do the work of inquiring into how meaning is made, especially with regard to colloquial language. Since these were spontaneous moments that required an immediate reaction, I tended to react as a disciplinarian, which is not altogether wrongheaded. However, when else can a teacher take up inquiry? What is served by waiting? Weren't these complex moments, rich with opportunity, that I sensed the threat in? I now see these as moments when I could react, but in a manner that would spark inquiry. However, to have the intellectual agility to respond depends on a few factors: knowledge of how best to respond depending on the goals of the instructor and how those responses fit into an overall classroom structure and curriculum.

More Violations

Neither my work as an ally in the GSA nor that in class seemed to be making any effect at times. Even in May, after we had spent almost an entire school year together, students were still crossing lines I had clearly drawn. During a unit on *Romeo and Juliet* with 9th graders, I raised the possibility of Mercutio being in love with Romeo. This was one of my attempts to include discussions of sexuality, but it was rather unformed. In response to a question, one student whom I will call Devin used the word *fag*. After the first two utterances, I asked him to stop. He said it again several times, and I said, very directly, "I need you to stop using that word." "Why," he said in apparent earnestness, "is it a bad word?"

I was exasperated. It was near the end of the school year. I was tired. I felt like I was the only teacher who ever reacted to this kind of speech and it made me angry. I had made it very clear that I found this kind of language personally distasteful, but had also explained how it was generally hateful, punishable speech in a classroom as well as nearly any professional social setting. I asked him to stay after class.

After everyone had gone, I sat next to him and asked if he knew that *fag* came from *faggot*. He said he already knew that a faggot was a bundle of sticks, and he also knew it was something he didn't want to be. I told him about some of the associations the word has—starting fires for burning heretics (including gays) as well as the fact that it conveyed hatred. I am not certain it is true, but I told the story (which I now understand to be apocryphal) about using gay people to fuel fires, including ones in concentration camps. It seemed to make an impact. He said, "I didn't know all that." His tone sounded apologetic, ashamed. Upon reflection, I feel bad, or more precisely, intellectually dishonest, because I know that the reason the word was offensive to me was less because of any convoluted etymology, but more because a student who was hostile toward gays was using it. When this kid said "faggot," there was fear, ignorance, and aggression behind it.

This vignette is an example of the fruit borne of only policing language and not inquiring into it. Perhaps if I had done more of the work of encouraging students to understand where hate speech derives its power from, this might not have come up at all. But the purpose of critical inquiry is not simply to stop this kind of speech; in fact it is to push through the places where there are silences. These can be useful moments, especially if students are asked to do some inquiry in response. Winans (2006) found that providing students with opportunities to question themselves and their roles in communities provoked dissonance that improved their understandings of their own power and the power of the communities with which they are affiliated. What kinds of strategies might I have employed to help Devin and so many students like him to understand that his affiliations, for example, as a young, straight, Black male in an urban setting, make his choice of words possible?

Moments like this one represented a threat to my hopes of being an effective activist, to being the kind of teacher I wanted to be—a change agent. My worldview was at risk at the very moments when I was trying so hard to enact it. I could understand flaws with power structures, but explaining what I understood had little effect beyond making myself visible as an ally. Students who did not share this worldview most likely saw me as a power figure to disagree with and resist.

My hope for moving forward is to sidestep this relationship by inquiring alongside students, structuring collective inquiry into communities of discourse. This might even include inquiring into hate speech. The prospect of asking young teens to inquire into hate speech sounds frighteningly full of pitfalls. But Winans argues that failing to talk about it, with particular respect to sexuality, limits critical thinking opportunities, ignores the realities of students' lives, and thus "supports and validates an unquestioned heteronormative environment" (pp. 105–106). Winans suggests a process of inquiry in which her students inquire into their communities of discourse and analyze them.

But teachers should not make students' comments in class an opportunity to put students on display. Inquiry into this kind of hate speech must happen in other ways, perhaps by looking at case studies and stories.

The End of the Year

There were a few times when students took up discourse related to LGBT identities in constructive ways. I'd like to think it was partly a result of my efforts, but that is not a conclusion I can easily substantiate. In the vignette that follows I think through how my student, Arthur, took an assignment and used it as a kind of discourse about sexual identities. While I was encouraged by the risks he took, I am concerned about whether his discourse was read in meaningful ways by other class members. From the beginning of the year, I thought Arthur might be gay. Although he never came out to me, there were signs—I am admittedly subject to the effects of stereotypes. Perhaps he never felt he had to come out to me. As part of the *Romeo and Juliet* unit the 9th graders were doing, Arthur did a multimedia scene adaptation. He used the ballroom scene and reinterpreted it into a scene at a decadent Lower East Side club featuring images of women kissing men, men kissing men, and women kissing women. It was intended to shock and challenge the class; he even said so in the opening scenes. It purposely featured nonstraight sexualities as being as good as if not better than straight ones. It even depicted Romeo and Juliet as having a vapid relationship based on looks alone. I was amazed; Arthur had been quiet and withdrawn all year in my class. He was a smart reader and writer, but tended to keep to himself. What, in the last weeks of school, made him do this? I thought it might make him vulnerable, so I was ready to come to his defense. However, when his piece ended, the class clapped. Many were smiling, shaking their heads in disbelief.

Why did Arthur take this stance, whereas before, during our many discussions, he kept his thoughts on sexuality quiet? If I can say my ally work came together at all, I will say it came together like this: Arthur felt safe to explore this idea in a public way and no one attacked him in class. That is, I expect that if he might have anticipated some resistance, and thus a threat, from students hostile to LGBTQ students he must have also anticipated support from me.

Even though I felt good about the fact that this discourse could happen, I do make a critique of how it fits into this overall narrative of my work as an ally. It is quite likely that students had come to feel comfortable in a stance of tolerance toward LGBTQ-related discourse, or that they simply found his presentation outrageous and titillating. In other words, he and I were having a discussion, but I don't know how that fit into a discussion for the whole class, or an entire year of challenging students to make sure they approached language and texts with a critical mind. Arthur had made a queered version of *Romeo and Juliet* that I found interesting, but there wasn't any impetus for the students to challenge or support his text. In fact, I could argue that I had created an atmosphere of tolerance such that challenging Arthur's presentation was off limits simply because it was so openly about LGBTQ identities. Further, I struggle to articulate what students might have learned by only watching his presentation. I recall that any discussion I tried to stir up afterward was met with halfhearted replies. I conclude that without a larger context of critical inquiry, I was successful in making space for talk about LGBTQ issues—engendering tolerance. But I hope for more, for encouraging the kind of learning that examines power, even my own as the authority figure in class.

Conclusion

Conspicuous within this chapter is a lack of enough direct examples of how to enact queer pedagogy in a secondary English classroom and how to plan for the kinds of threat I claim are so useful. In the time that has passed since the year I recount here, I have still struggled to find ways to foster critical inquiry in public secondary education. No single strategy that addresses homophobia and heterosexism is without problems, but I prefer the problems that an inquiry approach brings up to the problems of teaching tolerance—especially when, in public school, tolerance typically ends up being enforced by the uneven power relationship between students and teacher. To my thinking, this relationship implies, "Don't do or say anything that appears intolerant," but does nothing to transform students' thinking about sexual identities. James A. Banks's (1997) hierarchy of multicultural education leads me to think that properly addressing multicultural issues requires an inquiry approach to effectively avoid the "food and festivals" approach. While I am uncomfortable with lumping LGBTQ people in with people of differing cultures and ethnicities, the concept works via analogy here. Winans (2006) voices a similar concern: "the additive approach of inclusivity or celebration of difference tends to leave dominant cultural assumptions and their complex relationships to power unexamined. Simply put, changing the content of our classes does not necessarily impact our pedagogy" (p. 104). I extend Winans's argument: Allowing students to change the content does not necessarily affect our pedagogy either.

I began this year of teaching with a determination to be active in my pursuit of social justice with regard to LGBTQ identities in school. I had identified being an English teacher as an appropriate and important site for this work. My resolve to take risks was fortified by affiliating myself with a like-minded community—the Pink TIGers. And while the group was and still is a source of support—emotional, practical, and otherwise— there were large gaps in my understanding of risk and threat. Many of these gaps come from my being new to teaching and being new to the context in which I was teaching. In my analysis, a key component I was missing was a deep understanding of using an inquiry approach as a pedagogical tool for addressing LGBTQ identities. My assumption is that using an inquiry approach effectively in my classroom might have been an instructional support that gave students tools and context for address- ing LGBTQ identities within texts and communities of discourse. Also, it might have helped me begin to get to the heart of my fears, anxieties, and worries as a teacher. In fact, a realization I had in writing this chapter is that the things that kept me willing to take risks and endure the sickening feeling of threat was my personal proclivity for not shying away from risk (arguably a self-destructive drive at times!) and the knowledge that I had a community to support me.

In this chapter, I challenge my assumptions as I endeavored to be an activist teacher. I had gone into this school year hoping to have my stu- dents do the same. Without oversimplifying it, perhaps I and other teach- ers who want the same out of their students need to provide what I have been provided: an intellectual construct for challenging one's own ideas and a supportive community behind it.

References

Banks, J. A. (1997). Approaches to cultural curriculum reform. In J. A. Banks & C. A. M. Banks (Eds.), *Multicultural education: Issues and perspectives* (pp. 229–250). Boston: Allyn & Bacon.

Cohen, H. S. (Producer) & Chasnoff, D. (Producer & Director). (1996). *It's elementa- ry: Talking about gay issues in school* [Motion picture]. (Available from Women's Educational Media, San Francisco, CA.)

Fecho, B. (2001). "Why are you doing this?": Acknowledging and transcending threat in a critical inquiry classroom. *Research in the Teaching of English, 36*(1), 9–37.

Freire, P. (1970). *Pedagogy of the oppressed*. New York: Continuum Books.

Lee, A. (Director), Proulx, A., & McMurtry, L. (Authors). (2005). *Brokeback mountain* [Motion picture]. United States: Universal Studios Home Entertainment.

Mellor, B., O'Neill, M., & Patterson, A. (2000). *Reading fictions: Applying literary theory to short stories*. Urbana, IL: NCTE Chalkface Series.

Newman, L. (1988). A letter to Harvey Milk. *A letter to Harvey Milk: Short stories* (pp. 25–28). Ithaca, NY: Firebrand Books.

Winans, A. E. (2006). Queering pedagogy in the English classroom: Engaging with the places where thinking stops. *Pedagogy: Critical approaches to teaching literature, language, composition, and culture, 6*(1), 103–122.

6

Activist Work as Entry-Year Teachers

What We've Learned

RYAN SCHEY

ARIEL UPPSTROM

WE ARE TWO HIGH SCHOOL English teachers who during our 1st year of teaching made the decision to be coadvisors to our school's gay-straight alliance (GSA). Given that, as preservice teachers, we both questioned the viability and safety of social justice activism, we want to share our experiences with others who are considering taking a similar path in their own professional lives. Our story begins with the factors in our lives that motivated us to do this work. We follow by describing key factors that have allowed us to do successful activist work as 1st-year teachers, and conclude with advice for others who might also choose to engage in this work.

I (Ryan) do LGBTQ activist work because of the injustice and inequality I see around me every day, including exploitation and oppression targeting individuals and groups based on race, religion, social class, gender, sexuality, disability, and other categories of difference. As a straight White male coming from a middle-class Christian background, I feel a responsibility and drive to do whatever I can to change it. I believe that the most ethical way to respond is by using my privilege and resources in an attempt to reconstruct an unjust system.

Specifically, I do LGBTQ activist work because of the individual students I see at my school who come to me with stories of homophobic bullying. I do it because ally signs and GSA signs, such as fliers for meetings and rainbow stickers, are constantly defaced or destroyed in my school. I do it because of the student who comes every day to my study hall, where we talk about his trouble with homophobic parents or romantic interests. I do it because of the student who secretly passes me a note letting me know that my open ally stance helps him feel comfortable in my classroom because his mom is a lesbian. I do this work because, whatever their sexuality, so many of the young adults in my school never encounter a thoughtful or safe dialogue regarding sexuality. I hope to reverse this trend.

To be perfectly honest, I did not set out to do LGBTQ activism. Rather, the educational contexts in which I found myself had needs and provided opportunities to live out my social justice ideals through LGBTQ activist work. I student-taught at the school where Jill Smith (author of Chapter 8) teaches and, through the suggestion of Caroline Clark (author of Chapter 3), I sought her out and began attending meetings of the GSA she leads. Later when I became employed at my current school, the GSA needed an advisor because the previous one had just retired. The idea of actually making a choice to do this LGBTQ-activist work really never entered my mind. Instead, it simply felt like the natural result of my ideals.

As I (Ariel) began to pursue my degree at The Ohio State University, I was encouraged by my parents, who worked for equality for all people, to engage in social justice work. Through my English and women's studies classes, I began to see a glaring need for activism with regard to lesbian, gay, bisexual, transgendered, and queer (LGBTQ) rights. After receiving my bachelor's degree, I worked at an agency for runaway teens, where the majority of my caseload were teens who questioned their sexual orientation and were not accepted for this at home. With this experience, I found it necessary to return to education in order to create spaces for teens to feel safe and understood. In the Master of Education program at The Ohio State University, I found like-minded educators who encouraged me to strive for equality in education for all students, which led me to search for teaching positions where I could continue this type of work.

While interviewing for my current job, I discovered that the school needed a gay-straight alliance advisor for the following school year. Knowing that Ryan had accepted a job at the same school, it was not hard for me to turn down other jobs in order to pursue this unique opportunity. Although it was daunting to take on an unpaid, potentially controversial extracurricular activity in my 1st year of teaching, my background had taught me to go for what was important.

Despite our different backgrounds and motivations, we worked together as teachers, GSA coadvisors, and activists for a common goal: creating justice with respect to sexuality issues within education. Over the course of our teaching careers thus far, we have learned many important personal lessons as activists. We primarily write this chapter to share our reflections with others who would like to do similar work in their teaching contexts. However, what we have learned is grounded in our context and subjectivities; it is our story, not a program. The most important lessons that we learned are (1) the benefits of inquiry, (2) the importance of acting strategically, (3) the necessity of balance, and (4) the value of developing a support system.

The Benefits of Inquiry

Going into the district, we only knew the basics about the town and school. The town consists of 30,000 people, many of whom continue to uphold small-town traditions and ideals that, consequently, shape the values of the school. Since the town was originally an agricultural center, the importance of farming and religion dominates much of the politics in the area. However, most of this context seemed abstract to us as we began our 1st year of teaching.

We knew that the GSA had been in existence for a number of years prior to our being hired at this large, rural town high school. The most recent advisor had retired, but we were under the impression that the group was fairly established. We soon discovered that there had been very little advertisement or visibility of the group previously. Once school started, we placed fliers advertising the first GSA meeting for the year around the school. Immediately, we saw signs torn down. It shocked us how quickly students reacted to the signs. However, we continued to simply put more signs up until the first meeting. We also noticed an increase in graffiti. Janitors would point out derogatory graffiti in student bathrooms, and this allowed us to see the undertones of the school community and all the work that would need to be done throughout the year.

Prior to our first GSA meeting, students in each of our English classes asked what the GSA was, since they knew we were leading the group. We both took the time to explain the group and normalize it in our classrooms, but this was not easy. We felt it was important to answer all questions brought to us about the group no matter the amount of time it took because it was clear that students were simply uneducated about GSAs and gay issues. Although it seemed to initially take time away from the already hectic beginning of the year, we felt it was essential to be as visible and verbal about the GSA as possible.

We quickly discovered that we had underestimated the opposition to the group within the building and in the community. It was only through inquiry and by engaging with the staff and students who supported the organization that we were able to see where there were barriers and why. For example, during the 1st month of meetings, two supportive teachers came to the GSA meetings. They were not simply there for support but because they knew what we did not: There might be a great deal of opposition or conflict with our group. If not for their forward thinking, we may have run into more issues and resistance than we did. Also, it helped to have coworkers who could discuss with students in their classes events happening in the GSA. These conversations in classrooms beyond GSA meetings created more visibility and consistency in the school about expectations for all students regarding respect for LGBTQ people and related issues.

One of the first items on the GSA's agenda for the year was creating "Safe Space" signs for teachers to place on their doors so students would know where to come if there were issues of bullying or harassment in the hallways. The students then designed a sign, and an email was sent out to staff asking them to reply if they wished to have a sign. The GSA sponsored an Ally Day that would signify the putting up of Safe Space signs and teachers would be encouraged to wear rainbow ribbons to show support for the GSA. Early on, we were concerned about the Safe Space signs because it would be obvious to students the teachers who were not supportive and did not create safe spaces in their classrooms. We discussed this with each other and inquired about the issue with other teachers. With input from our colleagues, we concluded that students should know who was not supportive in order to protect themselves and secure help when necessary. Therefore, we proceeded with Ally Day.

Many teachers requested a sign and the day appeared to go smoothly, but we learned that there were underlying currents to which we were oblivious or that we thought we had addressed early on. By the end of the day, we were questioned about the appropriateness of the signs, and some colleagues asked if the school had decided to have LGBTQ issues at the forefront of the year's agenda. These questions felt confrontational, not merely inquisitive. After discussing these responses with some of our teacher colleagues, we discovered that nothing regarding safe spaces had ever been done by the GSA (or any other group) before, and some teachers were surprised by and even concerned about the GSA's mission. Given this history, we were particularly proud of our GSA members for seeing the necessity of overtly marking safe teachers to draw attention to the unsafe quality of the school.

It was only by questioning staff and students about these negative reactions that we were able to begin to be proactive instead of reactive as the year progressed. We feel it is essential for any teachers who choose to take on GSA advising in their 1st year of teaching in a district, or even early on in a career, to fully question and inquire into the motives and history in the school where they teach. If we had known the complete lack of visibility for the GSA during previous years, we would have been able to prepare the staff and administration prior to a number of our actions in order to create a more positive reception to student-led tasks.

We cannot claim that once we completed this first Ally Day we understood all the issues in the school and district, and many more sprung up as the year progressed and the GSA became more visible. Our main point here is to highlight the benefits of ongoing inquiry. It is essential to continue to search out information about one's school and district, and to learn about and from key players, such as teachers, administrators, and community members. In our case, if we had simply reacted to what appeared to be resistance instead of searching out the actual cause for concern, we may have created more problems for ourselves later on.

The Importance of Acting Strategically

We also learned that it is important to act strategically as LGBTQ activists. In no way does being strategic mean compromising personal values or giving up on certain issues. Instead, it recognizes that activists need to keep sight of the larger end goal and thoughtfully weigh options in decision making. We found this lesson a challenging one to learn because our personalities and dispositions make it difficult for us to let some issues go and to allow ourselves to be at peace when letting go is necessary. In addition, we often struggled to differentiate between battles that are worth fighting and battles that need to be left behind.

Our experience with the Day of Silence, a national effort in which students at individual schools across the country use silence to protest the silencing of LGBT people through bullying and harassment in schools, illustrates the difficulties we encountered when trying to act strategically. This event was important to our GSA for several reasons. First and foremost, our members saw the event as a public way to take a stand in our school with respect to LGBTQ issues. They also saw it as accomplishable; for them, it felt like an event that the GSA, along with other supportive students, could all participate in proudly and successfully. Next, it was an event in which the GSA had previously participated. The participants were unsatisfied with previous years, however. The event was not advertised, so even though the students participated, there was little public knowledge of the event or its rationale. For our 1st year, the GSA members saw the day as a culminating event for the group and thus worked to be more prepared and have a higher profile than previously.

The Day of Silence was also made important by the protests that grew in our community. Months before the day of the event, before we had even begun to discuss serious plans in the GSA, our high school and district began to receive phone calls, presumably from community members, complaining about the Day of Silence. Our principal discussed the calls with us, we provided more information about the day and our plans for the GSA, and collectively we had thought that the calls would die down. Just the opposite happened. As the event came closer, more and more complaints through phone calls, emails, and other means came in, many of them from enraged and grossly misinformed individuals from inside and outside our community. Individuals attacked the school for promoting a "gay agenda" and a "gay lifestyle," accusing the school of forcing children to believe a so-called liberal point of view on homosexuality. Parents threatened to pull their children from school during the day unless the event was banned and the pro-gay assembly was canceled (no such assembly was ever planned or discussed). Others complained about national gay organizations coming into our school (again, no such plans were ever made or discussed). Some complained that silent teachers would not be able to carry out proper instruction for the day (the pattern continues: no teachers were considering participating). Based on conversations with GSA advisors from other schools experiencing similar complaints, it appeared that a national conservative Christian organization was targeting the Day of Silence and encouraging local congregations to protest the event. Because of this fervor, the day took on even more importance for our GSA. It became a battle that was clearly worth fighting.

Initially, our principal and vice principals repeatedly stated their support for our group's participation in the Day of Silence. Strategically, we wanted and needed to work with our administrators, providing them support as they worked to understand and support us. To do so, we drafted email responses to questions and complaints, discussed with them how to respond to phone calls, and clarified the nature of the event and the group's participation. As the day approached and the complaints mounted, we suddenly were called to have a conversation with the assistant principal, who told us that the administration supported our group's participation in the event; however, we would not be allowed to advertise with posters, fliers, or announcements or publicly let the students and staff in our school know about it. We were limited to *word-of-mouth* promotion.

For us, this stance was unacceptable and absurd, as it negated the goal and purpose of the Day of Silence. Because we had the enthusiasm of the GSA and the support of our building administration, we felt that many factors had aligned and so were prepared to devote our resources to this battle. But even with these factors in place, we knew we had to act strategically. In the short term, we had to work for the approval to advertise publicly and participate. In the long term, we knew we had to work with our building administrators in navigating the community politics web between the school, central office, specific congregations, and community members. We were unwilling to compromise on public participation, but also realized the cost of a high-stakes zero-sum game where we burned the bridges of previously cultivated relationships.

We were not privileged to all of the conversations among our building administrators, district administrators, and community members that happened next, and so do not have all the details to share. What we did do was get in touch with all the allies we knew in the school and the district, explaining to them the situation and our stance. Each one of them told us that they could not find out who had told our assistant principal to deliver the message about the ban on advertising, and eventually the ban was dropped. However, there were still restrictions, such as a requirement to submit all advertisements for administration approval. Technically, this procedure applies to all postings made in the school, but we are unaware of any other times it was actually applied during the year. At this moment, acting strategically meant initially pushing hard to preserve the public nature of the Day of Silence, but then acquiescing to the bureaucratic hoops placed in front of us. While ideally all groups in schools should be treated the same with respect to the application of policy, strategically we were not at a time when fighting for this equal treatment would have been productive or meaningful for our activism. By fighting the bureaucratic inequities, we would have been focusing on a tangential, although ultimately important, issue.

After submitting our materials and receiving approval from our building administrators to advertise, we were elated and went into that month's staff meeting to explain the event and the day's procedures to our colleagues. However, we had assumed more school-level support than we would actually receive. As we had done with previous GSA events, we were preparing to distribute rainbow ribbons to staff members who wanted to show support of the day's antihomophobia and antibullying message. However, the administration quickly made it clear that any teacher showing visible support for the day would receive no support or defense if a parent, student, or community member complained.

After speaking with other allies in the district again, we initially decided that strategically the ribbons were a not a battle we could fight and win. We didn't know enough at that moment to find a policy or legal angle and we had less than 24 hours until the Day of Silence began. Despite our ambivalence and frustration with this conclusion, we accepted it and consoled ourselves with a vow to push further the next year. Colleagues then began contacting us to find out the district's decision and we passed on the message that teachers would not receive administrative support if they chose to wear ribbons. Many staff members threw this advice to the wind and wore rainbow ribbons despite this risk. We wore our GSA shirts proudly. For us, our initial concession showed us that we can easily misread and poorly estimate a situation, especially when attempting to act strategically, if in isolation.

Acting strategically has greater utility than merely avoiding the burnout of trying to do everything as an activist. By selecting key battles that will take on a larger symbolic importance, activists can stretch their resources beyond the specific moment. For example, one such battle we chose was refusing to accept homophobic language in our classrooms. We made this policy and its rationale clear from the start of the year. Language in and of itself is an important space where prejudices can be either performed and entrenched further or challenged and undermined. For this reason alone, challenging students' use of homophobic language in classrooms is a worthy cause to take up. Simultaneously, we believe that this practice was a symbol representing our basic position on homophobia to our students. Through this touchstone, many of our students understood that we were supportive of LGBTQ individuals and would not tolerate anti-LGBTQ words or actions.

At the same time, we recognize that because of our limited resources, we were not able to address every instance of homophobic language in our schools. While we both took strong stances in our classrooms, neither of us chose to fight the language battle in the hallways or at assemblies and pep rallies. With only a few minutes between classes and a new group of 30 students entering our rooms, we did not have the time it would take to contend with an anonymous student walking through the halls using homophobic language. Doing so would have been a disservice to our academic students and would not have meaningfully confronted the anonymous student's homophobia. Finally, we know that the time we invested in language policies came as a trade-off to some other element we might have addressed in our classroom. While we do not have a specific omission in mind, there are many, such as the dress code, that could function as placeholders. Nevertheless, we believe that, strategically, language policies are an important battle into which teachers can invest time. Ultimately, this trade-off and others like it all point to the importance of balance in a teacher's life.

The Necessity of Balance

In addition to the benefits of inquiry and the need to act strategically, we also learned the importance of having balance in our lives. As entry-year teachers and activists, finding and maintaining balance among all the areas of our personal and professional lives that 1st year was a challenge of paramount importance. From lesson planning to essay grading to department meetings to extracurricular clubs to professional development sessions to teaching evaluations, there are numerous commitments that pull teachers in many directions. It is easy to let one element become increasingly important over an extended period of time so that it dominates all other considerations. Doing so can lead an activist to the instability of skewed priorities and perceptions, diminishing the effectiveness of activism. Balance helps one to remain grounded, realistic, and optimistic. For us, this balance made our activist work possible.

In our professional lives, we needed to maintain balance in our roles in our school and district. Whether with the visibility of the GSA, the materials we used in class, or events such as the Day of Silence, we pushed the status quo in our school with respect to sexuality issues. We believe that contributing to the school community in other ways helped our activist work because we demonstrated our investment in the school's greater good and not merely our investment in our social justice perspective. Most important, we demonstrated our investment in the school in ways that the school recognized as valid and valuable. For example, Ryan spent significant time with other freshmen teachers working on curriculum mapping and the beginning stages of creating common formative assessments. For him, taking on this responsibility built relationships with others in the building and demonstrated a commitment to the school's academic goals, giving him more freedom to work with LGBTQ activism. For Ariel, contributing has meant working with the academic quiz team and being coadvisor to the freshman class, including running a mentor program. Together we took leadership in our professional learning community time, revamping the junior-senior-level groups in order to meet the district's expectations for this time. Overall, maintaining a balance in our professional roles and acting as *team players*, we earned more leeway in our activist work.

We found it important to have a balance in the output of our activism. Beyond our classrooms and school, we worked with our district's multicultural committee, taking on goals such as amending the language used in district policies (for example, the antibullying and antidiscrimination policies). This involvement helped us to broaden the scope and nature of our work. We now were able to connect with other colleagues in elementary schools, middle schools, and the central office in order to affect change in all the schools along with the district's direction overall. Our different results reinforced one another because progress on one front often affected the activity on another. For example, our work with district policy on the multicultural committee made us more prepared to respond to challenges regarding the Day of Silence.

The GSA was one place where the question of balance continually arose in multiple ways. Mainly, we often struggled to find a satisfactory balance between having the group be student-led while maintaining our goals. One of our central concerns with the GSA is to make the group relevant to the students' needs and desires. Another is to empower students to make positive social change. For us, it is essential to disrupt the traditional student-teacher dichotomy in order to accomplish these goals. To realize these abstract ideals, we planned to create a core of three officer positions in the GSA. These student leaders would be primarily responsible for planning the group's overall direction, leading meetings, and communicating with us about their needs and concerns.

To us, these concrete steps seemed a great way to move the GSA to be more student-centered; however, in reality, it did not initially work out this way. During our first year of coadvising the group, our officers were unreliable and took little ownership of the leadership role. Usually they did not attend officer meetings and eventually their attendance at GSA meetings started to waver. When they did attend and attempted to run meetings, the results were scattered at best. For example, during a meeting at the public library with other GSAs from several different schools, our officers led the group off task into personal gossip and inside jokes. Toward the end of an icebreaker game, one officer was bickering with another girl in the GSA. The conversation exploded when the officer screamed out, "Just because I had sex with you doesn't mean I wanted to date you!" to a room full of dumbfounded onlookers. At times, the officers would ignore the plans we had developed for a meeting. In some instances, they avoided personal ownership and responsibility by stating that the group had to do an activity because Mr. Schey and Ms. Uppstrom told them to do so. When we developed plans and strategies with the officers to address these issues, we rarely saw changes that lasted beyond a meeting.

Our troubles with the officers were frustrating for the GSA overall. We felt it was essential for the group to be student-led; otherwise it would lose much of its potential to be relevant for the students. At the same time, we did not want to see the group fall apart. When no officers showed up to a GSA meeting, we saw little choice other than to step in and lead a productive meeting with the members who did attend that week. When meetings went off on extended tangents and floundered unproductively, we struggled with our role. We felt it was important for officers to have the space to make mistakes and learn from them, but after a string of unproductive meetings that left members frustrated and discouraged, we felt compelled to intervene and keep meetings focused. However, we continually struggle with questions about when, how, and to what degree to intervene.

At the core of this struggle was the issue of balance. We needed to find a place where we could give students enough responsibility and leadership that helped them to take ownership over the group, but not too much responsibility so that they became overwhelmed and ineffective. In doing so, we tried to find a balance in the nature of our meetings. It is essential that students have time to socialize and build relationships at the GSA without the group descending into a gossip club. For the group to have a sense of purpose and direction, it needed to have outside objectives and goals, for example, creating "ally" signs for teachers, discussing LGBTQ young adult literature such as Bauer's *Am I Blue? Coming Out from the Silence* (1994, see entry in the Annotated Bibliography of this book), or making plans for screening *The Laramie Project* (Kaufman, 2001).

We have yet to find the right balance for our GSA and believe that it will always be a work in progress. In our 2nd year, we have used a similar approach with three core officers, but added in more commitment and structure. We drafted contracts with our officers, committing them to the responsibilities and obligations of their leadership roles, have regular officer meetings after school with them, and often meet with them during our all-school academic-assistance period. We have had much more success with this approach. Officers have made mistakes and some meetings have gone awry, but they have learned from these instances and have been committed to planning more effective meetings and giving the group more direction.

The Value of Developing a Support System

Creating and relying on a support system of colleagues and friends was one of the most important factors that allowed us to successfully do activist work as 1st-year teachers. A key piece of advice we would offer to others is, if at all possible, do not start a GSA alone. It is a very emotionally draining and time-consuming extracurricular. It is not similar to student government or tennis, because the issues involved frequently carry a great deal of baggage for people. We would not have been as successful with the group if we had not worked together. Not only were we coadvisors of the GSA; our classrooms were also next door to each other. This allowed us to see each other daily and discuss not only the tribulations of 1st-year teaching, but also the challenges we faced in addressing homophobia in our school. We each have a different approach to working with young people and react differently to opposition. The fact that we were able to immediately go to one another when a situation arose helped us to look at all sides of an issue, weigh the choices, and act more effectively than if we had been alone in the situations. For example, when we were initially told we could not advertise the Day of Silence, Ariel's immediate and passionate response was to go yell at someone at the district level. Ryan's immediate response was to reflect on the motivations of individual players

and seek a route to deal with those problems. After working through those emotions, we were able to talk with different individuals at different levels and put pressure on people instead of simply responding passionately. We have had students come to us who have problems with bullying, and we each have our own roles in dealing with the bully and the individual. It is this mix of "fire and ice," as Caroline puts it, that enables us to be more efficacious in our work.

It is important to note that having two advisors is not always easy. There is a difference between coadvisors and a leader and sidekick. We worked hard together to always discuss issues or ideas and work through them together to maintain a coadvising atmosphere. This also helped the students see that they did not have one leader to go to, but two, and that each had equal access to information in the group.

In addition to having a coadvisor in the GSA, we urge other activist teachers to create a network of like-minded professionals who wish to pursue the same goals in and outside the district. Since we knew two of the cofounders of the Pink TIGers, Mollie Blackburn and Caroline, from our graduate work, we were invited to participate in the teacher-inquiry group. This group allowed us to come together with experienced teachers who could look at our situations, which we were too close to see, and give their sound advice on how to respond. For instance, when we were invited to participate in the Multicultural Council, a group made up of staff from across the district with the shared mission to advocate for equity, we discovered the need to create policy for the district that included protection for LGBTQ individuals. After bringing this up on the Pink TIGers' email Listserv, Jill met with us and we discussed the ways in which she pursued these same policy changes in her district. The group also allowed us to vent to other teachers who knew where we were coming from on issues and could talk us through ways of maintaining our momentum for these issues without getting burned out. Without this outside release, we would not have been as effective. Therefore, we highly recommend searching for such groups as teachers begin this work in order to give support when it seems there isn't any close by.

Another component of this network is to find teachers, administrators, and parents in the district who support LGBTQ social justice endeavors. When we became visible in our school, other teachers came to us and offered support. They may not have always felt comfortable being visible to other staff members, but we knew we could go to them for assistance or insight into issues occurring in the school. However, there are those who were highly visible and reached out to us immediately. As we began our

1st year, we met a new 1st-year teacher in the district who had taught for 30 years at a neighboring district. His wife taught in our district at the middle school level. The moment we met her, we knew we had found a wonderful person and a wonderful resource in the district. She frequently had insight into different administrators' motives and history that we would never have understood without her knowledge. She was able to share stories with us from the middle school level that reinforced our drive to accomplish safe spaces at the high school level and to continue working with the Multicultural Committee (of which she was a member). For her, it was a relief to not be the only visible advocate for LGBTQ issues. Without her constant support, we may have felt alone in the district, but her connections allowed us to see the impact of our work at the high school. This network can also help with those teachers and staff who may not be as supportive. We were frequently notified by our network about individuals who seemed to be undermining the work being done to make the school safe, and this allowed us to address the issues with the relevant person to maintain a good working environment for all staff.

Our final piece of advice would be to search out other GSAs in neighboring districts and community-based groups that are working for LGBTQ rights. Once we discovered that a local gay-straight-Christian alliance existed in our town, we had access to a large group in the community who would make as many calls as those in the community who opposed what we were doing in the schools. This group also led us to connect to GSAs in five neighboring districts. By connecting to the other GSAs, our students were able to see that they were not alone. We set up monthly joint meetings with the other GSAs to allow the students to share experiences and support as well as to socialize with people their own age who supported them. Many of our students then connected to the GSAs through Facebook and MySpace, thus creating their own network of support. As advisors, students would email us about issues occurring in other districts, and this allowed us to support those advisors. These connections in the community and across districts created opportunities for us to seek out help when we were faced with opposition. Without these other sets of eyes, we would not have been able to see all the strings attached to the issues with which we were dealing.

It is important to have support when dealing with controversial issues in schools. Once we placed ourselves into networks, we were able to act as a support system for others and share our insight and experience. Throughout our 1st year advising the GSA, we were contacted by at least three other teachers in other districts in the state asking for advice on starting a GSA. We had an advisor and a student come to observe our meetings to see how they could use our model in their school. When we allowed ourselves to be visible in our community, we were able to help others become visible. It is only through this networking that GSAs and similar organizations can maintain momentum and achieve the goal of creating a safe learning environment for all students.

Conclusion

We understand the difficulty of being a 1st-year teacher and taking over a controversial extracurricular such as the GSA; however, we also know that social justice is at the forefront of many teachers' reasons for entering teaching. Therefore, we wrote this chapter to give tools to those who may be wary about taking on more in their 1st year. Our goal in writing this chapter was to demonstrate what to do and what not to do to the best of our knowledge. The task was never easy, but by inquiring into the district and the staff, we became more prepared to act strategically in order to reach necessary goals for the district and our students. Finding a balance in our personal and professional lives became indispensable as we faced 1st-year teaching evaluations and the stress of teaching full-time. However, we would never have survived if it were not for each other and the many support systems we came across and nurtured throughout our year. We would encourage others to follow our lead by engaging in inquiry, finding balance, and creating networks of support. Creating safe spaces in schools for LGBTQ students is a draining experience. If it is possible to head off some unnecessary distractions or areas of wasted energy, we hope that our advice accomplishes this task. By no means is our advice applicable to all situations or for all teachers, but it is a jumping-off point. We wish we had known what we know now. If we had, who knows how much more we could have accomplished in our 1st year?

References

Bauer, M. D. (1994). *Am I blue? Coming out from the silence.* New York: Harper-Collins.
Kaufman, M. (2001). *The Laramie project.* New York: Vintage.

7

Facilitating Visibility of LGBTQ Issues in Public Schools
Teacher Resistance and Teachable Moments

MINDY HALL

IN THIS CHAPTER, I DISCUSS MY COMMITMENT, as my district's international/multicultural coordinator and a teacher, to facilitating visibility of LGBTQ issues in public school, the resistance I have encountered in talking with teachers, the teachable moments I have seized, and the role of community in this work. Finally, I reflect on where my district is, where I see it going, and why.

Addressing LGBTQ Issues in Schools

It was spring 2008 and the school day had just ended. After a busy morning of doing research, making contacts, and taking care of daily business as my district's international/multicultural coordinator, followed by an afternoon teaching 2nd grade, I was preparing to leave for a local association meeting that, as president, I would be running. The meeting was scheduled to begin in less than 15 minutes so I knew I had to gather my belongings and head out the door. Just as I was grabbing my coat and bag I looked up and noticed a 6th-grade boy standing outside my multicultural office reading a poster that I had hung up earlier in the school year. "No homophobic remarks spoken here," it said. The young man popped his head into the doorway of my room. "What are homophobic remarks?" he asked of no one in particular. My eyes opened wide, certainly making me appear more alert and awake than I felt at that point in the day. I quickly averted my gaze away from the door and toward my teaching partner. "Oh, no," I thought. "How am I going to handle this?" My mind raced in a million directions. "I don't have time for this right now," I thought and then chided myself almost immediately, knowing I must answer this child's question; to make excuses would violate everything I stood for as both a person and an educator. A simple explanation came to me. "It's like calling someone gay," I said. "Oh," he responded with a quick nod of his head and walked away.

Although I recognize that the term *gay*, in and of itself, certainly does not constitute a homophobic remark, I also know from experience that when used by students in this school setting, it is homophobic. Indeed, all words referring to homosexuality are typically used as put-downs. For this reason, my response to his question seemed sufficient and, because of its clarity, a good one.

Addressing LGBTQ issues in school is daunting. However, as educators, we are there to provide information to all our students, whether we feel completely comfortable sharing the knowledge or not. It is imperative that we either give students the information they seek or help them discover it. By responding to the 6th-grade student with an "I don't have time for this" comment or attitude, I would have not only opened the door for him to ask the question of someone who might have answered with misinformation but I would have also devalued this young man and the knowledge he sought. The simple fact that I have this poster displayed in such a prominent place implies that not only is it a message I want to share with students, parents, and staff, but it is also one that I am ready and willing to discuss.

When it comes to being straightforward and talking about matters related to LGBTQ issues with elementary-aged students, I have always been willing to discuss, intervene, and answer questions. I know that in doing this I am taking a risk. After all, there are no hard-and-fast rules or directions explaining how to do this. I do know, however, that not to say anything, whether it be in response to a question, a discussion students are having, or a homophobic remark, is the biggest injustice of all. I am certainly aware that, in having these conversations and embarking on these teachable moments, parents, colleagues, and administrators might question my judgment. This is a risk I am willing to take. Throughout the 20 years of my teaching career, questions have arisen about how and why I teach reading and writing the way I do, the absence of behavior modification in my classroom, and why I rarely assign seats to my young students. These professional choices I make are solidly grounded in research, educational philosophies, and what I believe to be best for students. Thus, my classroom environment, teaching, and assessment strategies and other decisions I make as a teacher can be defended and explained without a problem. I do not see these incidences as threatening, but opportunities to share why I do what I do. The same goes for discussions surrounding lesbian and gay issues.

For example, during a discussion with a (noneducator) friend about addressing homosexuality in the classroom, she expressed shock and concern. "Why would you ever consider teaching about sex to 7- and 8-year-olds?" she asked. My head swirled with disappointment. "I'm not talking about sex," I told her. "I'm talking about relationships." I went on to say that heterosexuality is taught in schools on a regular basis. I explained that mainstream children's literature features heterosexual relationships, emergency forms typically ask for the mother and father's names (thankfully, in my district, that is no longer the case), and female teachers often have photos of their husbands or boyfriends on their desks. Heterosexuality, as the norm, is implicitly and explicitly taught in our classrooms and schools. How does this reality affect the child who has two moms or two dads? What does it do to the student struggling with his or her own sexual identity? What about the lesbian teacher who wants to display framed pictures of her partner on her desk? One of the most important roles of our schools is to create safe spaces for students. Not only are many schools not safe for LGBTQ students and students whose parents are LGBTQ, I will go so far as to say that teachers and administrators who do not teach about or discuss issues related to homosexuality create unsafe environments for these students.

Pink TIGers

Powerful incidents, such as the one described above, and ones I describe later in this chapter, led me to the Pink TIGers. I was eager to have professional discussions with others who were combating homophobia and heterosexism in school settings. I was interested to find out how these educators, in various surrounding school districts and university settings, dealt with resistance, embraced teachable moments as they occurred, and included lessons and literature related to sexuality in their teaching practices. Were there LGBT-themed units that they knew about that I could introduce to my district? Was anybody aware of districts that had included LGBTQ issues and literature in the elementary school curricula? Although the answers to these questions are still at large, the monthly meetings with the group have been very helpful. I have been introduced to many resources. Books have been purchased for the high school library. Recommended DVDs and books were purchased for the multicultural resource room.

Realities of Including LGBTQ Issues in the Classroom

Years ago, as a participant in a multicultural seminar in my district, I was given a priceless opportunity to watch and then discuss *It's Elementary* (Cohen & Chasnoff, 1997). The film documents curriculum-driven lessons and units focused on, and inclusive of, sexuality in elementary and middle school classrooms. The video displays educators facilitating and reflecting on lesbian and gay–themed lessons. Students are shown brainstorming, discussing, questioning, and commenting on topics rarely talked about in classroom settings (see entry in the Annotated Bibliography of this book). At the time, the segment that focused on a 3rd-grade homosexuality unit had the greatest impact on me as a teacher of 8- and 9-year-olds. In a whole-class setting, the teacher began the unit by encouraging students to brainstorm all they knew or had heard about the topic. Without judgment, the teacher asked for clarification when needed but all thoughts shared were included on the growing web at the front of the classroom. This lesson gave me possibilities for my own classroom. Could I actually teach a similar unit in my school district? I wasn't so sure. If, in fact, I were to plan such a unit, would I have to get administrative permission to teach it? Those questions have crept in and out of my mind for many years now.

As my district's international/multicultural coordinator, I implement the school district's international/multicultural education program through one-on-one work with teachers (lesson/unit planning, teaching resources, professional development plans), teaching a four-part seminar series (for college credit) to educators in the district, disseminating articles/readings on culturally relevant teaching practices and current events related to diversity, leading the district's international/multicultural literature discussion for staff (4 times a year), and collaborating with the curriculum director to infuse culturally relevant teaching throughout the district's curriculum (K–12). In this position, which I've been in since 2006, I have had the opportunity to show *It's Elementary* to some of my colleagues. During the summer of 2008, after one such viewing, a teacher asked, "Could I teach a unit like one seen here in my classroom?" I responded with a "No, it's doubtful." I went on to explain that this is a question I have been struggling with for years, the desire to teach explicit lessons related to homosexuality as part of a classroom unit. I know I would first have to seek permission, and I am fairly certain it would be denied.

The freedom to teach such a unit, grounded in state standards and district curricula, does not even seem to be the reality in a district such as mine, where emergency forms have been purged of heteronormativity; sexual orientation language was included in the recently adopted district antibullying policy; and a committee of educators, parents, and students was created (in the late 1990s) to view LGBTQ literature and resources to be included in school library collections. In a district whose multicultural professional development program was established in 1990 and, from the start, has included sexuality under its "multicultural umbrella," I am confused and saddened that more headway has not been made with regard to teaching formally about LGBTQ issues. If not here, where? If not now, when? If not here and now, why?

As the multicultural coordinator, what power do I have to make districtwide changes? Although I try to make districtwide change through all components of my job, I most consistently do so in the seminar series by showing films such as *It's Elementary* (Cohen & Chasnoff, 1997) and *20 Straws* (Gjestvang, 2006)—a documentary featuring teenagers to 20-something-year-olds talking honestly about their experiences as LGBTQ young people in local area schools (see entries in the Annotated Bibliography of this book). Sadly, though, the number of educators affected by these films is very small because taking part in the international/multicultural professional development seminars is completely voluntary.

In an attempt to include sexuality as part of a diversity and equity discussion with colleagues, the international/multicultural district committee shared an article, "20 (Self-) Critical Things I Will Do to Be a More Equitable Educator" (Gorski, 2003), with my teaching staff. Several months earlier I had run across this piece (edchange.org) while doing research. I was so moved by it that I shared it with the committee. The committee decided that this article should be shared with staff members in all five buildings in the district. My building principal was quite supportive and immediately scheduled a teaching colleague of mine (also a longtime member of the international/multicultural district committee) to run an upcoming monthly after-school staff meeting centered around the Gorski article.

Because the staff was known to be vocal, I felt certain that conversation would be open, honest, and productive. The discussion on topics such as centering classroom discussions around students and their interests, reflecting on how a teacher's identity affects the way he or she experiences others, and understanding the relationship between intent and impact was, for the most part, strained and awkward. I was shocked. An under-the-breath, but loud-enough-to-be-heard, comment was made by a colleague saying that diversity education should be a responsibility of parents, not schools. At one point a staff member brought up the topic of homosexuality being discussed in the classroom. Many teachers kept quiet. One or two posed their opposition to just such a lesson, be it planned or a teachable moment. Two or three of us were quite vocal in stating the importance of just such dialogue in the school setting. The bottom line, I said to my colleagues, is that this has nothing to do with religion or politics but the safety and knowledge acquisition of all students. But it seems that many educators cannot separate the religious piece from the classroom. Many don't seem to realize or understand the importance of infusing sexuality in one's teaching. Including race, religion, and culture is becoming more mainstream in curriculum development and classroom teaching, but the inclusion of LGBTQ issues, sadly, is still considered off limits to many.

Teachable Moments

Constructed curricula inclusive of LGBTQ issues do not exist in many (if any) public school districts in the Central Ohio area. However, that should not preclude the opportunity to take advantage of teachable moments. Excellent educators know that these diversions from original lesson plans often provide the most powerful and meaningful learning of all. But what if these paths take us down roads some see as "bad," "evil," or irrelevant? When the words *gay* or *lesbian* are used in the elementary school setting, how is it handled? Do teachers choose to ignore homophobic remarks? Do they make up excuses for not answering questions or discussing comments about LGBTQ people generated by students? I had such an experience. What it taught me was that even though these situations seem complex and difficult, they really are not. As an educator I must be responsive to the questions and concerns students are bringing to the classroom. To do anything else is to do them a disservice. To do anything else is to cheat these young people of valuable and pertinent information. To do anything less is to look your students in the eyes and lie.

It was late October 2004 and my 3rd-grade students were involved in creatively and artistically expressing themselves in response to an assignment related to our current unit of study. As is often the case in my classroom, noncurricular-related conversations ensued. Functioning as a student at this point, I was working on my own unique project using the artist's tools of paper, pencil, crayons, and watercolors. Sitting with several boys, at a far table, back toward the window, facing the classroom door, I was both a part of and apart from the surrounding conversations. I focused as much on my tablemates as I did on the other students in their self-selected groupings, scattered throughout my classroom.

"He's raising the gas prices." "He wants to make America safer." "He's bad . . ." "He's good . . ." "I'm voting for . . ." began to bombard me from all parts of the room like baseballs being hurled from an automatic pitching machine. I decided I had better attempt to make contact with this barrage of verbalized thoughts, rather than allow them to fly off in all directions, leaving misinformation and half truths soaring through the air.

I had purposefully avoided the topic of the upcoming presidential election, knowing I was far too passionate about it to lead an objective conversation with my 8- and 9-year-old public school students.

"Okay," I boomed, causing all chitchat to cease, all artistic expression to stop, and all eyes to focus on me. "We need to talk about the upcoming election." The teachable moment had arrived; I could either go with it or sidestep it. I faced it head on. I walked into the hall, quickly returning with a large sheet of paper. I pinned it to the front board and wrote: "What we think we know about George W. Bush and John Kerry," making a two-columned chart, purposefully writing the president's name first, in an attempt to conceal my prejudices.

Students returned to working on their projects, raising their hands if and when they had something to contribute to the chart. As secretary, I wrote the words just as they were spoken, much like the teacher in *It's Elementary* (Cohen & Chasnoff, 1997). When all ideas had been generated, I began to discuss each in turn.

"President Bush doesn't want gay people to get married," I read to the class. This was Mark's comment. Good for Mark. I noticed a few students shifting in their seats; others peered around the room uncomfortably, some looked at the floor, and others continued with their work. "How's she going to handle this one?" I imagined several students asking.

To explain both Bush's and Kerry's positions on gay marriage, I needed to be certain my students knew what it meant to be gay. Amid some nervous 3rd-grade giggles and surprised expressions, I dove in like a pelican plunging into ocean water for a tasty fish. "To be gay means that if you're a man you love another man or if you're a woman you love another woman in the same way some of your moms and dads love each other." Expressionful "Oohs" seeped out of the quietness like toothpaste oozing out of an almost empty tube of toothpaste.

"That's gross!" "That's sick!"

"Why?" I asked.

Nobody seemed to have an answer.

I continued in what seemed a different direction, to ease the tension and confusion some of my students were exhibiting. "How many of you know 3rd graders who are excellent readers? They knew how to read before they started kindergarten and can now read really hard stuff. It's as if they were born ready to read." Many hands shot up. "How many of you know talented soccer players who can play the game more expertly than others at their same age?" Several kids nodded; others raised their hands. "How many of you recognize gifted artists, kids who just have this amazing ability to draw?"

"Like Olivia and Aaron," somebody said.

"Do you agree that people are born with certain traits?" I questioned. Again, there was agreement either through expressions or words. "If you're a talented singer, artist, athlete, or writer, is it by choice or were you born to be this way?" I inquired. There were mutterings, but the consensus was that, yes, indeed, one was born with certain gifts or qualities.

"Gay people are born gay," I proclaimed. "It's not a choice. They don't necessarily know it when they're young, but at some point they realize it. Some of you seem to think it's weird or gross. I have to tell you that I have many good friends, both men and women, who are gay." Surprised looks. "Think about this—what if, at some point, you discover that a friend or family member is gay? Do you say, 'Ooh, sick!' and abandon them? Or do you say, 'It doesn't matter 'cause they're still the same person I've always known and loved?'" Silence filled the space around us.

I looked around the room, realizing it was probably time to step down off my soapbox. Curiously, however, I noticed one little boy who was sitting in a different spot from where he had been when I started my "sermon." Yes, he was still in the same blue chair. However, instead of being directly in front of my desk, about 12 feet away from where I was standing, his chair was directly to my right, approximately 3 feet away.

Why had this "speech" attracted this young man to me like metal to a magnet? How did it happen that he slowly narrowed the gap between us without notice? Had I sent him the message, "I'm an ally," "I am safe," "I understand that everyone is not the same, and I value the differences?" Was his physical relocation a silent "Thank you?"

Although I described that being gay is not a choice, it truly isn't as simple as that. Taking into consideration that I was working with 8- and 9-year-olds and knowing that homosexuality is often portrayed as a choice (and nothing else), I wanted my students to realize that there is more to it than that.

As the students present for this conversation grow older, will some reflect on my message, remembering that early in their school career there was a teacher who was "safe"? That there was a teacher who respected those seen as different? That there was an adult in their past who knew that to be gay, lesbian, bisexual, or transgender is virtually the same as being born with artistic, linguistic, or athletic gifts? The follow-up documentary to *It's Elementary, It's Still Elementary* (Chasnoff & Chen, 2007), suggests they will (see entry in the Annotated Bibliography of this book).

Was there backlash form this teachable moment? No. Had there been, I was comfortable and confident holding my own ground explaining what I said, why I said it, and how the teachable moment presented itself. I have had these explanatory discussions with colleagues many times over the years. There is not always agreement, but there is a willingness to listen.

Simple choices send the message of safety in quiet, understated ways that are clear and recognizable to students. Posters displaying messages of inclusion, posted quotations of people from many cultural groups, artwork that captures images of respect and tolerance, literature written or illustrated by and for a variety of groups, and symbols on visible stickers and buttons need to be purposefully and prominently displayed in our school, classrooms, and offices. If nothing else, this alone lets others know who you are *and* what you stand for.

Although many might argue that elementary-age children are far too young to know their sexual identity and to be exposed to information about LGBTQ people and issues, and are not even interested, I beg to differ. Children are much more sophisticated in their thinking than some might assume. They seek out truth, are open and willing to learn about various perspectives, and are often aware of what is in the media. Creating safe spaces for all students must be a priority for teachers, schools, and districts.

Community

In spring 2007, Kristen, one of the high school's guidance counselors, contacted me, interested in information about LGBTQ people that was housed in the district multicultural resource center, as well as information about high school gay-straight alliances (GSAs). She said that a student had come to her wanting to start a GSA and asked her to be the advisor. In addition, this student had recently come out as being gay himself. Kristen was hoping to have young adult literature and resources to share with this young man but, as a new counselor to the district, found the LGBTQ resources in her office limited to a few old pamphlets. Several meetings occurred during the spring, setting the foundation for the GSA that officially began in fall 2007. I was included in these planning stages, as was a local youth center leader who heads up a facility that helps to create safe environments for LGBTQ teenagers. Additionally, I invited Kristen to a Pink TIGers meeting. She has been a part of the group ever since. With the expertise and experience of Pink TIGer GSA advisors, the GSA has created a mission statement and received valuable advice about dealing with obstacles faced by other local GSAs. The monthly discussions not only have led Kristen to important decisions with regard to advising the high school student group, but also have provided her with ways that students can get involved outside the district. Information about teen book discussions, and copies of the necessary books, have been provided to those teens seeking to get involved. Community-wide activities for LGBTQ youth have been shared with Kristen through Pink TIGers meetings as well.

Conclusion

Does the existence of a GSA open doors for LGBTQ-themed lessons and discussions to become realities in classrooms? At this point, there is no way of knowing. Given the support of several central office administrators, the existence of a district multicultural education program, and the eagerness of a handful of high school students, the door could be opening just a crack. In such a small district (about 2,000 students) it stands to reason that, as the GSA raises awareness through education and activities with high school staff and students, information will filter down to the middle and elementary schools. I assume, however, that this process will be slow. Given the discussions that transpired during an elementary school staff meeting (mentioned earlier in this chapter) and conversations I have had with the district curriculum director, I cannot predict if and when explicit teaching about LGBTQ issues will become a reality in my district's schools. Although the curriculum director has been supportive of including sexual orientation as a "category" under the multicultural umbrella since the inception of the district's international/multicultural education program and has been instrumental in creating a proactive group of educators, parents, and students to review LGBTQ-themed literature for our school libraries (to prevent parents from attempting to ban literature once it is placed in the libraries), she refers to sexual orientation as "the last holdout." She went on to explain that although it is seen as "politically incorrect" to speak of another's race or religion in derogatory terms, many still find it acceptable to speak in such terms with regard to sexual orientation. This "reality" (if it is that) frustrates us both.

My work to move my district to one where LGBTQ issues and literature, at all levels, can be explicitly introduced by teachers has a long way to go. If I am to succeed in doing so, I am certain that the Pink TIGers will be a big part of that success.

References

Chasnoff, D. (Producer & Director), & Chen, S. (Producer). (2007). *It's still elementary* [Motion picture]. (Available from Groundspark, San Francisco, CA.)

Cohen, H. S. (Producer), & Chasnoff, D. (Producer & Director). (1997). *It's elementary: Talking about gay issues in school* [Motion picture]. (Available from Women's Educational Media, San Francisco, CA.)

Gjestvang, L. (Director). (2006). *20 straws: Growing up gay* [Motion picture]. (Available from Youth Video OUTreach Collective, Columbus, OH.)

Gorski, P. C. (2003). *20 (self-) critical things I will do to be a more equitable educator.* Retrieved June 18, 2009, from www.edchange.org/multicultural/resources/self_critique.html

8

Overcoming an Identity of Privilege to Support LGBTQ Inclusivity in School

JILL M. SMITH

I HAVE BEEN AN LGBTQ ALLY—a straight person who advocates for LGBTQ individuals—and a member of the Pink TIGers for several years. My work as an ally has included starting a gay-straight alliance (GSA) in the large, suburban high school where I teach and advocating for LGBTQ-inclusive policies in my school district. The consequences for this work have at times been dire, leading me to lose, but ultimately regain, my job. Reflecting on the challenges I have faced in my role as an ally has forced me to confront, recognize, and work against my privileged identity. In this chapter, I will characterize the challenges I have faced in my role as an ally and discuss how these challenges connect to my positions of privilege in both the school where I teach and, as a White, straight woman, in the wider world.

The challenges of my process as an LGBTQ ally have been characterized by several things: (1) recognizing the difference between privileges and privileged identities, (2) building upon that knowledge by recognizing how the ways identities are privileged may work (or not) in a variety of heterosexist and homophobic school spaces, and (3) acting on this awareness to help transform those spaces. I believe that this process of recognizing and overcoming a privileged identity is crucial in ally work, and is an essential part of the work of every educator. I share my story in hopes that doing so will help other straight ally educators to become more conscious of the roles of privilege we occupy and to guide us as we work for social justice.

Recognizing a Privileged Identity

An important part of recognizing the difference between privileges and privileged identities calls for a reorganization of long-standing beliefs about what it means to me be a *successful* teacher. I had always viewed having privilege and being successful as linked in the following way: Rewards were based on my level of achievement. However, the fact is that individuals who occupy privileged identities are awarded actual and symbolic prizes by society regardless of the ways they succeed—or fail— as they move through the world. As an ally, I see my work as being with and for students whose identities are often not privileged, particularly in schools. My goal was to change my school by making it safer for my LGBTQ students. However, maintaining that institutions such as schools employ an equitable reward system simply reifies the notion of privileges as markers of success. Thinking more critically about the ways that reward systems were based on privileged identity rather than on feats of success/ achievement required me to examine my own complicity in supporting the system that I wanted to redefine.

One of the most difficult things for me to recognize was the way that I had been granted privileges in my school, such as curricular freedom and access to material resources, because I was a straight, White, middle-class, married female. These aspects of my privileged identity had been opening doors for me my whole life, but I had never been aware of it. I first remember recognizing my own privileged identity when I saw myself reflected in the actions of individuals with whom I had not previously identified, namely White male athletic coaches. One particularly salient incident of this recognition occurred when I decided to informally track a couple of homophobic comments that I had heard many times around my school: "Hate the sin, not the sinner," and "I don't agree with that lifestyle." I noticed that these comments appeared to be made, unchecked by some teachers, whenever the issue of homosexuality came up. I began to think harder about the kinds of statements that were permitted, if not supported, within school spaces. What kinds of people were allowed to make which statements? In what ways were their words supported? Was *I* one of those people? How had *my* statements been supported? I began to realize that within reasonable professional and personal limits, I rarely curtailed what I said or where I said it in the building. In ways similar to my colleagues' comments on sexuality, sweeping statements about students based on perceptions of socioeconomic status, such as "He's the kind of kid who will end up in jail if he's not careful," or "It's no surprise the kid acts that way; look at who the parents are," felt, unfortunately, familiar. I believed that my speech and actions were supported because I was a hard worker and mostly knew what I was talking about. What I realized, however, was that I could see a good portion of myself reflected in the heterosexist or homophobic actions of colleagues whom I considered privileged. For all my stake in doing the best job that I could as an educator, I had removed myself from seeing my own complicity in creating and maintaining an environment that only served particular students, particularly those who identified as middle-class and heterosexual. By not recognizing my own privileged identity, I had been blind to ways in which I had been perpetuating class-based stereotypes.

One particular blind spot for me was in privileging certain texts in my classroom, namely those that did not include LGBTQ authors, themes, and characters. This kind of exclusion was not fair to any of my students, whether they identified as gay or not. Recognizing my privileged identity, both in the school and in the curriculum, allowed me to see how much more work I could do as an ally by consciously working toward LGBTQ curricular inclusion. Working toward LGBTQ curricular inclusion, not incidentally, is not some kind of lone "agenda," it's simply making explicit a particular kind of agenda—adding on to the many, shifting agendas that have been in place since the beginning of civilization. In my case, it allowed me to make my work as an LGBTQ ally more explicit in my overall work to teach for social justice.

Recognizing the Consequences of a Privileged Identity

While recognizing my privileged identity was challenging, understanding and owning the consequences of this identity was even more difficult, for a couple of reasons: 1) whether or not I recognize and own them, society recognizes visible markers of my identity, such as Whiteness, middle-class-ness, and heterosexuality, regardless of my level of awareness or allegiance to these identity markers; and (2) I was caught off guard by the extent to which the rules of my performance of these identities influenced the scope of the social justice work I was able to do.

These difficulties were illuminated as I made a fledgling effort to consciously capitalize on my identity by trying to address inequities in my district's discrimination policies. When I learned from a colleague that

LGBTQ students and staff were not protected by any of my district's anti-discrimination policies, I assumed that I could use my privileged identity to advocate explicitly for LGBTQ students and staff in the district. I began emailing a school board member in an effort to find out why this kind of exclusion was allowed and to push for more inclusive language to be added. Despite initially welcoming exchanges with the board member, my best efforts failed. As the conversation about policy language progressed, my access dwindled in terms of the number and length of email responses I received. Ultimately, the conversation stopped altogether.

What I gleaned from this experience was that my privileged identity as a straight, White woman and established educator facilitated my gaining audience for continued conversations with a school board member despite my clearly stated intent at the outset: I was advocating for LGBTQ students and staff. My actions were recognized as being too far out of alignment with my previous and *sanctioned* behaviors to allow for me to continue to be heard. Unlike the *successful* teacher work I had done for many years in and around the school, my work on behalf of LGBTQ students and staff was not valued or supported.

Two years later, I transferred to a newly built high school in the same school district. At this time, my privileged identity and status in the district were still sound enough for me to help a couple of great kids start a GSA at this new school. For a long time, though, we felt that very few people wanted our school to have a GSA. Thinking back, I see that we were being silenced whenever we tried to move forward with integrating ourselves into the emerging community of our new school. Most often this looked like nonsupport or avoidance, and for a year, we were not allowed to start the club at all. However, unlike my experience with the board member, this silencing felt immediately stark and explicit. One example of this was when an administrator censored our announcements. Once the group was established, rather than saying, "gay-straight alliance," the students reading the morning announcements were told to say "GSA." While this abbreviation may sound incidental rather than intentionally censorial, the requirement to use it occurred in the fall following the year in which we had not been allowed to start the club under *any* title and when not many people at the time even knew what the acronym GSA meant.

Working with young people to start a GSA does not come with the rewards that typically appear when one initiates nearly any other kinds of activities for students—academic clubs, theater groups, service organizations, and so forth. My actions were instead compelled by several key events:

- A female student whose older sister had been brutally attacked for being a lesbian had approached me to ask about starting up a GSA.
- A male student slipped an anonymous piece of writing onto my desk. The story was about two high school boys who, despite their love for each other, are miserable because they live with both the emotional and physical dangers of being outed.
- A fellow TIGer shared a story about something that happened in her district. The senior class president, a popular kid active in both church and school activities, and a few of his friends had written "FAG" across a drama student's car, adding the finishing touch of tossing a dead cat onto the hood. She talked about how there were no consequences, despite witnesses, for the crime because the boy who had been victimized and his parents refused to pursue it for fear of further violence. A local TV station promised to publicize the story and offered to mask the boy's voice and darken his face as he was interviewed, but the threat was too great, and the story was not made public.
- During a class discussion, one of my male career center students training to be a police officer stated that he would delay his response time to calls if he perceived the caller was gay.
- Ohio voters approved Issue 1, which banned same-sex marriage in the state.

Opportunities to acknowledge these kinds of events and the ways they affect safety are, unfortunately, abundantly available to every educator. But as my students and I sought opportunities to work against these and other forms of homophobia and heterosexism in our school and community, we found ourselves shut out by our building administrators, and hence, our school. In retrospect, our resulting outrage and defensiveness were probably attributable to the way people further positioned us as a group of outsiders.

I became conscious of my identity as a marginalized staff member and used this awareness to delve into our school and district handbooks to search for how, exactly, systemic exclusions of LGBTQ students were allowed. As I engaged in this research and used this knowledge to advocate for my students as the GSA advisor, I also worked harder to make my classroom teaching and English curriculum more explicitly LGBTQ-inclusive and antihomophobic by explicitly confronting students who used terms like, "That's so gay" in my presence. With each of these moves, my identity shifted away from being labeled a *good teacher* to being the one who was labeled as *always talking about gays, liberal,* and *feminist.* A couple of parents called to complain they did not like my "agenda." Another parent accused me of discriminating against male athletes because I did not like his son's "you're such a fag" jokes in the hallway. Perhaps most unsettling, many of my colleagues remained condemningly silent during my *Can-you-believe-how-ridiculous-this-is?* rants in the staff mailroom. These experiences stood in stark contrast to those I had experienced as a service learning teacher and National Honor Society advisor at my former school. Up until my work with the GSA, no one had been troubled by the way I defined civil rights. How is it that my work now had an agenda, yet, when teaching *To Kill a Mockingbird* or Elie Wiesel's *Night*, no one had ever said, "She's always talking about Blacks and Jews?"

Despite these challenges, my GSA students and I were oddly comforted by these events. They affirmed our felt need to have a GSA and do this work in our school. Our presence helped to flush out that individuals in our building were homophobic and that their homophobia was infringing on students' and staff members' rights. Proof felt exciting because it meant a truth we could point to so that other people would be outraged and would sit down or stand up in protest. Perhaps we then would, as bell hooks (hooks, 1990) inspires us to do, use our marginalization as a "site of resistance" as well as a "site of repression" (p. 342). As it turned out, we did use our eked-out space as a site of resistance, but we had to wait another 2 long years before our proof would serve to rally others in the building.

Using Awareness of
Privilege for Institutional Transformation

After recognizing and owning my privileged identity, and the possibilities and limitations it afforded me as an ally, I've begun to look more critically at the extent to which I've been enacting this role. What did *ally* mean? Had my enactments of ally been carried out in the ways that I'd intended? In ways that were best for the students? What did the future of the kind of work I was doing hold? Gloria Anzaldúa observes that unifying labels can create hazards. When discussing one of the limitations of the "unifying" concept behind queer theory, for example, she notes that "at times we need this umbrella to solidify our ranks against outsiders," but then also states that "even when we seek shelter under [queer], we must not forget that it homogenizes, erases our differences" (Anzaldúa, cited in Johnson, 2005). One thing that occurred to me was that in my efforts to help the GSA build and maintain safer spaces for LGBTQ students in our school, I had become too comfortable using "we" when talking about our GSA. Yes, I had been marginalized in the building; but my Whiteness, straightness, and adult status still allowed me to experience this marginalization in a more privileged way than was possible for my LGBTQ students. Distinguishing the times that "we" should be limited from those times when it is necessary, I feel, was crucial to the transformative process. Kurt Fuoss observes, "While it's one thing to permit talk about homosexuality, it is quite another matter to permit a homosexual to talk" (Fuoss, cited in Spurlin, 2000).

Without the support of the TIGers and opportunities for reflection, I doubt that I would have noticed that I had been taking too much ownership over the GSA. These realizations were concretized during a panel presentation by many of the authors in this book at the National Council of Teachers of English (NCTE) convention. Specifically, I noticed the different ways we were received during our presentation based on our identities as gay, lesbian, or straight; biracial or White; male or female. Seeing how audience members related to different members of our panel more than others helped me to see that we needed more kinds of GSA leadership representatives. I never wanted to take narrative authority from LGBTQ students and staff members, or for the rainbow sticker on my door to mean that I was the spokesperson for all things gay in our building. But the labels I was acquiring and the comments I was fielding from parents and colleagues—be these positive or negative—suggested that things were moving in those directions. As a countermove, I tried to listen more to students and to lesbian and gay staff members in our building and community rather than always being the one who was doing the most talking. While this kind of move in hindsight seems obvious, I think the difficulty I had doing this earlier may point to the absolute degree to which privileged identities are hegemonically present and reinforced in school institutions. Even though I saw myself as marginalized because of my work on behalf of LGBTQ students and staff, because my voice was still the strongest among our group (as a White, straight, middle-class person), I had been reinforcing the good-teacher privileges I enjoyed but had wanted to break away from in the first place.

Another key part of what I see as the process of using awareness for transformation occurred the summer prior to my scheduled return to my full-time teaching position. After taking a yearlong sabbatical to continue my graduate education, I wound up being involuntarily transferred into a traveling position that entailed teaching in four different classrooms between two middle schools. I heard rumors that some administrators "didn't want me in the building." Members of my English department tried to intervene on my behalf, but the involuntary transfer had been authorized in secret. I imagine that the crushed feeling I had was a small sampling of what some of my LGBTQ students experience much of the time, but with fewer options. The knowledge I had of other teachers of core courses who had been involuntarily transferred into traveling positions was this: All of them had been stigmatized for some kind of perceived personal or professional failing, and consequently, their reputations as teachers were seriously blighted. A couple of them, reading the writing on the wall, simply quit. I became aware that competency, tenure, and union membership can be nearly completely eclipsed by a homophobic administrator.

I connected with our union president, who put me in touch with our union lawyers, but since "no contract language was violated" they couldn't help me. My husband and I decided to hire an outside lawyer. There had to be some law against what had happened, hadn't there? Homophobic retaliation? Slander? We didn't even know how to name it. I spent several days looking for a firm that would take my case. As it turns out, there are no laws in Ohio against *heterosexist discrimination*—a term I picked up from one of the lawyers. Thinking that I could at least appeal to the ethical sense of my principal's bosses, I got a list of names and numbers from our union president and started trying to make appointments with higher-ups in the district. Because it was summer and, I suspect, because of the nature of my complaint, getting appointments was difficult. After 2 weeks, I was given the opportunity to tell my tale to our assistant superintendent, who listened sympathetically. I gave him copies of letters from my colleagues who had advocated on my behalf. "Doesn't this transfer seem a little unethical?" I suggested. "I've never even been late to work." He said he would "check into" the situation and get back to me. When he called me back he shared that he had talked with my former principal, but only said that the option of hiring whomever was deemed best suited to *any* open position belonged to administrators. Later, I learned to recognize that this kind of generalizing language can be used to create the illusion that nothing awful is going on. It's not discrimination if it can happen to *anyone*.

The night the school board was scheduled to formally confirm new appointments and hires, my husband and I dressed in suits and went to the district school board meeting. Our union president had advised against making a scene. I suspect that our presence in the front row let everyone know that future scenes were not out of the question. Looking back, I feel that this is another time when my privileged identities were evident. I was a White lady, husband in tow, who was on the verge of throwing a huge fit. Recognizing that my fit would have a larger audience because of my skin color, marital status, and sexual orientation did not occur to me at the time—I felt that my predicament was evidence to the contrary. In retrospect, however, I see how in the weeks that followed, my access in the community was not cut off in the ways it might have been had I not in some ways retained a privileged identity. For example, the school board president met with me and then advocated my case to the superintendent, the union president kept in touch with me daily, and several of my colleagues were constantly supportive.

Even so, I feel it is important to share a few details about my experience during this time. Although making these details public is not easy, I do so as a means of speaking to the issue of relativism: If being silenced affected me, as an adult, in terrible ways, what does silencing kids do to them? What becomes of LGBTQ students when we create and sustain environments that cause them to withdraw or drop out?

One of the worst parts of this period was that no one I asked would take up the now advisorless GSA. One teacher said outright that she was afraid she would lose her job. I felt very defeated and wondered if I still belonged in the Pink TIGers. I considered quitting teaching altogether. The situation seemed impossible. All these things felt as though manifestations of realizing that my work as an inclusive teacher and on behalf of LGBTQ students and staff was not valued—that I was not valued.

The day before the students were to show up for fall quarter I was reinstated in my old job. At the time, it seemed that my reinstatement was the result of a coming together of three avenues of resistance. First, the school board president had taken up my cause and had advocated to the superintendent on my behalf. Second, my lawyer filed a sexual discrimination complaint against the principal and assistant principal through the U.S. Equal Employment Opportunity Commission (EEOC). Although *sexual discrimination* was a misnomer, it was the only option we had, as there are currently no laws in the state of Ohio against discrimination resulting from one's sexual orientation or against heterosexism. If I had been from an un-protected class, been a White gay male, for example, I would not have had a case. The final area of resistance came from the staff. There had been par-ticular interest in the assistant superintendent's generalization of the hiring process. The notion of "It could happen to anybody" had served to a certain extent as protection for the district, but was threatening to staff members. Even if people didn't approve of my ally work or of our GSA, the idea of an administrator being allowed to transfer a teacher because he did not like her was threatening to everyone. If it could happen to anyone, other teach-ers certainly did not want it to happen to *them*. So, at 3:00 p.m., the end of our 1st teacher workday in August, I got a phone call from the union presi-dent, who had met with the superintendent, the assistant superintendent, the board president, and my administrator, and I got my job back.

Upon reflection, I see now that my reinstatement was not simply a re-sult of the avenues of resistance that came together that summer; it was that the avenues themselves came together because of *the ways I was per-ceived*. My privileged identity as a White, straight, married woman didn't disappear in the way I thought it had. As part of my renewed privileged identity, I found that I had a lot of support from the staff. My principal ignored me, but I found that I could do things without feeling that I had to ask. One move I made was incorporating even more gay-themed texts into the regular curriculum of all my classes. The Pink TIGers had devel-oped book lists that we could use in our classes, and with a grant funded by NCTE, several of these books were purchased. Earlier in my ally work, I began the process of bringing gay-themed texts and signs into my class-room; however, I typically only had one copy of a book, and usually these titles were not as visible as they could have been. After my reinstatement, I gradually became bolder, putting novels out in the classroom where *all* students were likely to see them. I moved these texts higher up on my bookshelf, to the ledges of the chalkboards, and to the place where stu-dents always seem to most gravitate: my desk. The increased visibility of gay-themed texts in my English classroom made a positive impact almost immediately. I began to see more student-initiated conversations about homophobia being brought up during class, and in the school as a whole. Student language became less homophobic and inclusive of LGBTQ peers. For independent reading circles, for example, gay and straight students selected books that explicitly reflected gay-themed material with little or no outright prompting. Our librarian even purchased several LGBT-themed young adult novels, such as *Boy Meets Boy* (Levithan, 2003) and *Hero* (Moore, 2007), on the basis of student requests.

One of the most memorable examples of the transformations that occurred at this time was in my students' final exam portfolios. For their exam, 11th- and 12th-grade English students had to design their own class curriculum by compiling a list of books, poems, movies, and posters that they felt were important for high school kids to read, see, and experience. Out of 55 students, 23—nearly half—chose to include texts they perceived as working against homophobia; of that half, four different groups chose to include more than one LGBTQ text; one group chose three texts; and one group of students chose *five* different gay-themed or antihomophobic texts. The students presented their portfolios publicly, giving extensive explanations for all their choices. I did not require LGBTQ-inclusive texts, or any others in particular, to be included in the portfolios. Although the students made this move on their own, I assert that the difference was in the way I presented the assignment, if not the way I shifted my pedagogy. LGBTQ was no longer a talking point, but rather a part of my lived experiences. In the field of narrative study, some scholars assert that *story* is a "fundamental instrument of thought," or something that is "fundamental to cognition" (Kumashiro, 2000; Ryan, 2007). If this is true, I like to think that with their LGBTQ-inclusive curricula my students have begun a transformative story within our school, perhaps even a metanarrative, which will help to implement new, more inclusive ways of thinking of our community.

Another example of transformation came in the form of work by a colleague and me on getting explicit language that would protect LGBTQ young people through our district's antibullying policy. Ohio House Bill 276 (Candisky, 2007) required all school districts in Ohio to submit antibullying policies and procedures to the Ohio Board of Education prior to 2008. Although the state's original model policy had included reference to "verbal taunts, name-calling and put-downs, including taunts based on ethnicity, gender, religion, sexual orientation or other protected and/ or individual characteristics" (Candisky, 2007, p. 15), the state ultimately decided to strip all enumerated language in favor of a more generalized statement. This shift occurred after some administrators complained that the language of "sexual orientation" could "make some school officials uneasy" (p. 7). Representatives for the state pointed out that individual districts had the option of adding enumerated language to their own policies. I knew that my district would be required to have some kind of policy in place before the state deadline and to do so we would have to have a committee. With the encouragement of the Pink TIGers, I felt secure enough to ask to be included.

The district's antibullying committee decided to adopt the state model without adding enumerated language. None of the district's committee members were given the opportunity to vote on the adoption, and it was simply decreed by the two highest-ranking committee members. Two of my English teacher colleagues and I attempted to get the decision reversed, but to no avail. The district school board voted to accept the state's antibullying policy, without enumerated language, as their own. Despite this setback, we did gain backing at the building level in the spring of 2008 by presenting a report on the policy omissions to two of the three high school site councils in the district. I feel that this move was significant in playing a part in gaining the support of our new superintendent, who, from the beginning, articulated full support for the addition of LGBTQ language to district policies. This kind of support was unprecedented in my experience. He didn't need to read the report my colleagues and I had written for our site council presentations, or the notes I had taken during the antiharassment committee meetings. He said there was no need, adding, "It's just the right thing to do."

Continuing to Work for LGBTQ Inclusivity

While my story is unique, it does suggest some key issues that other straight ally educators might consider in their work for social justice. A first step involves becoming more conscious of the roles of privilege we occupy based on identities we may hold as White, straight, married, adult, middle class, or a combination of these. Kevin Kumashiro (2000) asserts, "Schools need to be and to provide helpful spaces for *all* students," adding, "Educators need not only to acknowledge the diversity among their students, but also to embrace these differences and to treat their students as raced, gendered, sexualized, and classed individuals" (p. 28, my emphasis). If we are to best serve our students, we as educators cannot ignore that we, too, are gendered, sexualized, and classed individuals. Progress that is made or lost in the name of social justice for LGBTQ students depends on the level of recognition we have for our own privileged identities, recognizing how these identities work in the context of school spaces and acting on this awareness to help transform those spaces so that they can be safer and more equitable for everyone.

References

Candisky, C. (2007, July 11). Anti-bullying policy OK'd. *The Columbus Dispatch.* Retrieved June 18, 2009, from http://www.dispatch.com/live/content/local_news/stories/2007/07/11/NEWSTATEPOLICY.ART_ART_07-11-07_B1_QP78JVB.html

hooks, b. (1990). Marginality as a site of resistance In R. Ferguson, M. Gever, T. T. Minh-ha & C. West (Eds.), *Out there: Marginalization and contemporary cultures* (pp. 341–343). New York: The Museum of Contemporary Art.

Johnson, E. P. M. H. (Ed.). (2005). *Black queer studies: A critical anthology.* Durham, NC: Duke University Press.

Kumashiro, K. K. (2000). Toward a theory of anti-oppressive education. *Review of Educational Research, 70*(1), 25–53.

Levithan, D. (2003). *Boy meets boy.* New York: Knopf.

Moore, P. (2007). *Hero.* New York: Hyperion.

Ryan, M.-L. (2007). Narrative. In D. Herman, M. Jahn, & M.-L. Ryan (Eds.), *Routledge encyclopedia of narrative theory* (pp. 344–348). New York: Routledge.

Spurlin, W. J. (Ed.). (2000). *Lesbian and gay studies and the teaching of English.* Urbana, IL: National Council of Teachers of English.

9

Choosing to Stay "In" and the Significance of Race for Lesbian Teachers in Urban Classrooms

ANETTE MELVIN

A S A MEMBER OF THE PINK TIGers, I appreciated the fact that the intersection of racial and sexual identities created tension (as described in Chapter 10) that forced us to reexamine the mission of our group. As the only member of color in this group, I was pushed to think about multiple identities in complex ways, sometimes with frustration, but always with support. It was this tension, however, that provided the catalyst for this inquiry to explore the significance of race and how it impedes or encourages teachers' decisions to come out (or not) in schools.

Over time, as the Pink TIGers continued to meet monthly, I continued to wonder if other teachers had a similar interest in the significance of race and sexuality in education. I was aware of other gay and lesbian teachers in my district. Some I knew personally; others were friends of my friends. I wondered whether some of these educators shared my concerns or at the very least could provide different perspectives. When the Pink TIGers agreed to submit a proposal of our inquiries at a national conference, I decided to take that opportunity to explore the educational lives of one lesbian teacher representing each educational level—elementary, middle, and high school—who perhaps shared some of my sentiments about coming out to students.

My inquiry into the lives of other gay educators whose beliefs and perceptions about race influenced their perspectives on teaching and learning is discussed in this chapter. My hope is that my story alongside theirs will provide some insight into how racial identity dominates, at least to some degree, the decisions we make regarding students' learning and society's view of what is normative.

My Story

> I have often felt like I am several people, not in the multiple personality kind of way, but in the personae kind of way. It's not that I haven't wanted to be one, it's just that it's been impossible. I've always had to choose between being whole and being intelligible, being whole and being loved— between the desire to "be" and the desire to "be with." My body is not simple; it forces people to think about uncertainty: Is she black or is she white? Is she gay or is she straight? Where are the lines? (Phillips, cited in Kumashiro, 2001, p. 2)

I was born in a small town outside Schweinfurt, Germany, in 1967. The product of an interracial relationship between a White German woman and an African American soldier, I was raised by my maternal grandmother, since my mother worked in the city and my father left shortly after I was born. Being the only Brown child in this small town and in my school created an awareness of difference that was always present. Even if I wanted to forget, there were subtle and overt reminders from family and others. For example, arguments with my cousin ended abruptly when he referred to me as a *"neger,"* which translates as "nigger" and was used quite casually among many Germans. Or, when my grandmother and I would go out in the city, strangers often commented on my light skin and "good hair." I suppose these comments were meant to be compliments— though I assure you they were not. There was something odd about receiving that type of attention. Nonetheless, because I only knew of one way of being, I completely embraced a German culture that prided itself on a strong sense of cultural White identity. Because of my limited understanding of other cultures, including my own as half African American, I was ignorant of the nationalistic attitudes that many Germans had toward those who did not resemble the White-skin-blonde/brown-hair mold of perfection. What it means to be biracial in a German society did in part lead to an identity crisis for me. As such, when asked, "What are you?" my response was always, "I'm German."

My first memory of having contact with any person of color was not with my father. Because he left shortly after I was born, the only information I had about him was that he was Black and that he was a police officer in the United States. (I met him for the first time when I was 16 and had only spoken to him once prior.) Even so, it was as if everyone else knew who my father was without "knowing" who my father was: simply put, they knew he was Black. The other African American soldier in our small community was a family friend. My mother told me that when I was about 3 or 4 years old he picked me up and I cried because apparently I was startled by the darkness of his skin. According to her, she was quite embarrassed when I inquired about his "dirty skin." Perhaps it was because representations of the Other were limited. Films and literature, including children's books, often highlighted stereotypical features and behaviors. For instance, the old *Tarzan* movies portrayed Black people with cannibalistic tendencies; in literature, children's poems such as *"Zehn kleine Negerlein"* (Ten Little Negroes) had images of dark-skinned people with big noses and lips; and there was *Struppelpeter* (Messy Marvin), whose unkempt appearance was always represented by a brown-skinned individual. As a person of color whose self-image was often defined by comments and perceptions of others, I couldn't help but think that the stories or films about racial minorities somehow implicated me. In other words, sometimes I wondered if people honestly believed that people with darker (non-White) skin were unkempt and cannibalistic!

At age 10, everything familiar to me changed. My mother married a White American soldier and we were soon given orders to move to El Paso, Texas. The thought of leaving all my family and friends was exciting because I thought it finally meant not feeling that I was the only one. Yet it was also frightening because I was entering a world with an unfamiliar culture, a culture I had only seen and come to know through German television, featuring American shows. Interestingly, television shows in the United States were very helpful in my learning the English language, but did little for my identity and cultural development as a woman of color. For example, *The Electric Company* and *Sesame Street* were instrumental in the acquisition and development of my English-language skills. Whereas shows such as *The Jeffersons* and *Good Times* featured people of color and were quite popular, in my mind these shows did little to help me identify with an African American identity that resonated with or even slightly resembled my lived experiences. Popular during the 1980s and 1990s, television programs like *The Dukes of Hazzard, Love Boat,* and *Friends* featured no people of color or just one or two as supporting cast, not as lead actors. Unquestionably, one of the most successful shows in television history was *The Cosby Show,* which shattered all stereotypes of Black people, yet was criticized by some Blacks and Whites because it was believed to be unrealistic for a Black doctor and a Black lawyer to be married and living in one household. Representing a Black family in this manner was monumental because it illustrated the diversity among African Americans; furthermore, it was certainly more representative of the kind of life my father lived as a Black citizen of the United States.

Although I was still somewhat unclear about what it meant to be biracial, I knew I wasn't White. I suppose that was obvious to most people, especially my classmates, who often thought I was White and in moments of confusion casually asked, "What are you?" when I did not quite fit into an identifiable racial category. The idea that I was racially and linguistically different began to take its toll in my quest to just be me, whoever that is. Why was it so important for others to identify me? What is/was it with this country's obsession with race? What could be perceived as innocent curiosity in identifying my racial identity felt more like trying to justify who and what I am. Because I didn't have a strong sense of self, I chose to disclose my cultural, rather than my racial, identity: "I'm from Germany." I think this response, although true, also gave me permission to remain naive about what it means to Black in the United States. Furthermore, I felt a sense of relief because I no longer had to justify and address my non-White identity.

You're What?

After graduating from high school in 1986, I attended college on an athletic scholarship at a predominantly White university in Ohio. My naïveté about non-White cultural identities did not matter much initially. My abilities on the court and in the classroom were much more important to me, my coaches, and my teammates. The fact that there were only a handful of African American women on the team during my 4-year career spoke to the lack of recruiting efforts of African American women at a predominantly White university. Although I knew I was a woman of color, I'm not sure I ever said it out loud. I was quite comfortable with the perception people may have had of me. I liked that they wondered, "Where is she from?" Again, I could easily respond with, "I'm from Germany."

Nothing could have prepared me for what was happening as I began to explore my sexual identity more honestly. Although there was a general perception that a significant number of college female athletes were gay, most of my teammates were not; in fact, we only had one openly lesbian player and although her sexual identity was known, I never felt comfortable enough to talk to her about my own struggles. As such, I kept my sexuality hidden and continued to date men. I also continued to listen to hateful comments about my teammate, yet I never spoke up. Knowing what others said and felt about homosexuality forced me to remain closeted for far too many years.

Although difficult to admit, I finally acknowledged my attraction to women shortly after graduation. I was very careful whom I told; first, I didn't think it was anyone's business and, second, I could not even say it out loud: "I'm gay." The two words that had brought on so much angst later felt so liberating. My career in education was just beginning, and I certainly did not want parents and students to question my intentions or effectiveness as a teacher. No one, including colleagues, friends, and family, knew about my relationships with women. I began to tell stories about why I did not have a boyfriend. A new circle of friends became my support system, and I no longer had to hide my gay identity from them. However, I was still constructing a heteronormative identity at work and with most of my family, although I now question how "invisible" I really was. Remaining silent and telling lies, I thought, were my best options because discussions about homosexuality were often politically charged and religiously driven. I simply felt that I did not have the energy, language, and courage to speak up and to come out.

Today, I embrace my sexuality, and I am able to have conversations without worrying about being the "only one." I no longer fear the question "What are you?" whether racially or sexually. Yes, I have a stronger sense of self. However, in reflecting on those times when I struggled with issues of race and sexuality, I had to realize and accept that (1) I am a woman of color and no matter how I speak, what I wear, or where I live, some White people will make comments about my race, yet rarely their own; (2) I am attracted to women, yet the fear of coming out paralyzed me for a period of time . . . so I didn't; (3) I believed that I had to live in silence about whom I dated if I was going to have a career in teaching; and (4) even though I don't have White privilege, I am privileged for having light skin and "good hair" in the minds of some African Americans.

The Value of Stories in Critical Race Theory

To make sense of our lives, we tell stories to try to make meaning, just as the story above helped me make sense of my life. Stories or narratives are often used as a frame for analyzing teacher knowledge, perceptions, beliefs, and attitudes (Clandinin & Connelly, 1994; Doyle, 1997; McEwan, 1997). Furthermore, narratives help us make connections to our current position, our past experiences, and our future goals. As O'Brien and Schillaci (2002) remind us, "Narrative is often the spark that illuminates our professional lives because stories have the potential for reflection and growth" (p. 27).

However, it should be noted that narratives have not always been acknowledged as legitimate forms of representations in education and elsewhere, particularly from and about people of color (Matsuda, 1987). An earlier legal movement referred to as critical legal studies (CLS) challenged and critiqued "mainstream legal ideology for its portrayal of U.S. society as a meritocracy" (Ladson-Billings, 1999, p. 212). However, they did not think to include racism in their critique, thus prompting a logical outgrowth now known as critical race theory (CRT) because legal scholars of color were dissatisfied with the CLS movement to "provide pragmatic strategies for material and social transformation" (p. 212). As such, the use of CRT, according to Parker and Lynn (2002), provides a legal theory of race and racism that would finally expose the way they operate and affect "the education and lives of the racially disenfranchised" (p. 8). Used as a methodological tool, while also providing a better understanding ontologically (or how we see the world) and epistemologically (concerning ways of knowing), CRT evolved not only as a way to present narratives or storytelling as "valid approaches through which to examine race and racism" (p. 10) but also through legitimizing narratives by showing various interpretations that justified an ideology of racism against African Americans and other racial minorities (Delgado, 1989). According to Parker and Lynn (2002), the goal of CRT is threefold: (1) examining race and racism through narratives and storytelling and acknowledging them as valid approaches, (2) eliminating racial subjugation while recognizing race as a social construct, and (3) *acknowledging the relationship between race and other forms of domination* (my emphasis added).

Last, the use of CRT in examining the significance of race on sexual identity disclosure provides a theoretical framework not only for my story but also for the narratives of the three teachers discussed later in this chapter. Furthermore, by employing a narrative approach to tell my story and theirs from a critical race perspective, my hope is to present them with the assumption that the stories had "the capacity to contain and entertain within it contradictions, nuances, tensions, and complexities that traditional academic discourse with its expository stance and more distanced impersonal voice cannot" (Cochran-Smith, 2004, p. 83).

Being a Gay Woman of Color in Elementary Education

Exploring the power of narrative or storytelling has helped me embrace my racial/cultural and sexual identities professionally and personally. Subsequently, it has also created a quandary that just continues to raise more questions, yet seems to provide few solutions. For instance, I recognize the growth I have made in terms of teaching and learning, and how I see the world overall—sometimes still with what Du Bois (1903) has referred to as "double consciousness," that is, "this sense of always looking at one's self through the eyes of others" (p. 3). Nonetheless, even though I am not currently teaching in an elementary classroom, I still wonder how disclosing my sexual identity to elementary-age students would have mattered.

My struggle of whether I should have disclosed my sexual identity to my elementary school students, I believe, has to do with the idea of relevance, especially as it relates to academic achievement in today's high-stakes testing environment. In other words, to what extent would my disclosure positively affect the academic success of my (former) 5th-grade students, for example? In addition, was it not possible for me to remain closeted and still be an effective teacher? This is not to suggest that I would have avoided talking about same-sex families or "gayness"; I am suggesting that to come out as a teacher in an elementary school classroom is a personal decision, one that even now I am not sure that I would make.

What is certain is that my students saw me as a person of color. Occasionally they even asked, "Are you mixed?" As an elementary teacher I felt that my primary responsibility was to teach my students everything they needed to know academically in order to succeed in 5th grade and to pass all required standardized tests. The idea of incorporating social justice issues or even occasionally engaging in culturally relevant pedagogy was not a priority in my classroom or in my school. The emphasis was on raising test scores, because we had fallen under the umbrella of "academic emergency." In part, as a member of the Pink TIGers and in writing this chapter, I have been forced to reflect critically on my years as a teacher. Although my identity as a woman of color who is gay occasionally influenced how, what, why, and whom I taught, I could not out myself to my students and risk letting them see me as anything but "normal." I thought then that my racial identity was far more important in terms of getting students to identify with me, as well as learning the curriculum in a relevant and meaningful way. In fact, Agee (2004) explains that most African American teachers bring "a desire to construct a unique identity as a teacher. . . . She [or he] negotiates and renegotiates that identity" (p. 749) to meet the objectives and needs of her or his classroom. Finally, my racial identity was certainly important to my principal, who asked me to make sure that the district office was aware of my identity as "Black/ African American" to ensure that our building met its quota for minority staffing.

On a professional level, I think I will always struggle with how much of my personal life needs to be disclosed in an elementary environment, including sexuality. While there seems to be no definite answer, I will continue to be in a quandary about what it means to be Black, female, and gay in elementary education. How can the intersection of two or more identities coexist without the domination of one over the other? In pondering this question and perhaps trying to come to some conclusion, I came across Lorde's (1999) chapter in *Dangerous Liaisons: Blacks, Gays, and the Struggle for Equality*:

> Within the lesbian community I am black, and within the black community I am a lesbian. Any attack against black people is a lesbian and gay issue, because I and thousands of other black women are part of the lesbian community. Any attack against lesbians and gays is a black issue, because thousands of lesbians and gay men are black. *There is no hierarchy of oppression.* (p. 307, my emphasis).

An Inquiry Into Race and Sexuality

This inquiry, which was originally intended to describe the dilemma many gay teachers face regarding their decision to remain closeted in schools and the impact it has on student-teacher relationships, resulted in a deeper understanding of the confluence of race and sexuality in education. I found that each teacher's racial identity, as well as the identities of students, staff, and parents, whether African American or White, played a significant role in their decision not to come out at work. The fact that middle or high school students were older had no influence on their decision.

The reality is that these two contentious identifiers, race and sexuality, affect teaching and learning in a number of ways (i.e., curriculum, pedagogy, efficacy, etc.). The following section is intended to illuminate the quandary of three lesbian teachers whose racial identity influenced, to a large degree, their decision *not* to come out in the workplace.

The Classroom Teachers

Tonya, Donna, and Deneen began their teaching careers in predominantly Black urban communities and were still teaching in such communities when I conducted this study, although they have all switched schools more than once. All have said they would not want to teach in other communities. They represent a diverse group of women in terms of race, religious beliefs, and grade levels. Tonya is an African American female in a kindergarten classroom; Donna is a White female teaching 9th-grade Algebra I; and Deneen is an African American female teaching 7th-grade language arts/reading. They represent elementary, middle, and high school teachers who have shared their passion for teaching with me.

I conducted individual, semistructured interviews with each of the participants. Each interview was recorded, and I took detailed notes during each session. All have more than 11 years of teaching experience, and at the time of this writing Tonya and Deneen were both working on their master's degrees in education. (They have since completed their degrees.) It is worth noting that, according to these teachers, they are all considered to be strong educators by students and staff, they are all well liked by students, and each enjoys a fairly strong sense of efficacy.

Just as I believed that my silence had a chameleon-like effect by allowing me to blend in and be perceived as "normal," or straight, so did the teachers who agreed to share their stories. They, like me, chose not to reveal their sexual identities to students and staff, because they could not see the relevance of coming out in schools. In addition, they felt that their racial identities played a significant role in their decision, because they worked with a predominantly Black student population, whose members in their minds were more homophobic than the rest of society. I should note that my work here is not to explore (the lack) of validity of their claim, but rather to respect their perceptions and the influences their perceptions had on these women's lives. The anticipated backlash all thought they would receive and the heteronormative narrative constructed by the staff and students in many ways precluded them from challenging homophobia and heterosexism in their schools and in their classrooms.

I purposefully selected the three participants because I knew they were not out at work, but were out to family and friends. As Clarke (1999) pointed out, Black lesbians and gay men may have been "subjects of curiosity . . . [but] they were accepted as part of the community" (p. 41), which may explain why these teachers felt more comfortable with coming out personally but not professionally. What I was not aware of, however, was the degree to which race influenced the decisions they made regarding heterosexism and homophobia. For instance, Tonya, the kindergarten teacher, identified as a Black woman (not as a Black, gay woman), but felt race was not a factor at all when thinking about disclosing her sexuality. What may seem a contradiction, because I make the argument that race, at least to some degree, influenced their decisions not to come out in the workplace, is more about Tonya's naïveté about the significance of race when others see her as an African American teacher who also happens to be gay. Her own issues with internalized homophobia seem to flow into other areas of her life. When asked if she usually identifies as gay or lesbian outside the school environment, she simply responded with, "I'm just me, Tonya. Why can't I just be me?"

Similar concerns were also shared by Deneen, the 7th-grade language arts teacher. She believes her identity as an African American woman would resonate more with her students and staff than would her identity as a gay woman. As noted earlier, Agee (2004) pointed out that most African American teachers want or need to construct identities that resonate with their students so that the former can meet the objectives of their classrooms. When given the choice between dealing with a case of racism or a case of homophobia in school, Deneen preferred addressing racism because of the fear of being implicated or confronted about her own sexuality. "I just don't want my kids to see me that way," was a major concern for Deneen when asked about coming out in the workplace. Her internalized homophobia could very well be attributed to the strong influence of the church or to the (perceived or real) homophobia that she believes already exists in the Black community. Or it could simply be, as hooks (2000) explains, the vocal and outspoken ways that many individuals in Black communities express their antigay sentiments (see entry in the Annotated Bibliography in this book.) Furthermore, she believed that disclosing her sexuality would breach the trust she had established with her students and staff. Even when that trust included some of her students confiding in her about their own struggles with sexuality, she felt she could not "out" herself. Acknowledging that there are few positive, Black, gay people (regardless of gender) who would understand the difficulties of Black, gay youth trying to come out, and perhaps serve as role models, Deneen said she was not ready to be that role model for her questioning or out students.

Finally, Deneen also pointed out that because she does not fit the stereotypical profile of what many people think a lesbian *should* look like, she found it easier to keep that part of her identity hidden. Believing that the mostly African American parents and staff would create a negative atmosphere not only for her but also for her nephew, who is a student in her building, she did confess that she had been out at her previous building, where the majority of the staff were White. She explained that they seemed more accepting and less judgmental. Some gay educators of color are more comfortable acknowledging the significance of race in education, yet are more reluctant to interrogate sexuality, especially in the workplace. The battle between confronting racism and homophobia put Deneen in a position of having to choose one form of oppression over another. Unfortunately, as Kumashiro (2001) reminds us, as we try to challenge one form of oppression we often unintentionally contribute to other forms of oppression. That is, though it may be impossible to hide one's gender or racial identity (for example, a female experiencing sexism, or an African American being the target of a racist comment), the disclosure of one's sexuality still remains a matter of personal choice and can be masked or hidden in many situations.

Donna, the high school Algebra I teacher, also acknowledged race as relevant to her not being out to her students and staff, but in a different way. When asked to what extent her racial identity influenced her decision to not come out, she stated:

> Being White and coming out is worse. I already feel judged by many staff members because I am a strong teacher. I think they're intimidated and threatened by me. So bringing up a hot topic like homosexuality would not work.

She admits to experiencing a tremendous amount of guilt when some of her students come to her to discuss concerns or issues about their same-sex partners. In response, Donna tries to offer support without "outing" herself. Donna's need to construct a heteronormative identity had more bearing on her being a White teacher and a single mother than on being a gay woman.

Interestingly, the racial makeup of Donna's staff was fairly even in terms of Black and White. However, she realized that being in a minority-majority environment created racial awareness that was not visible in her life outside school. Donna's inability to see her Whiteness as power and privilege, even in a predominantly African American setting, illustrates the shame and guilt many Whites feel when confronted with issues of race and racism. For instance, when Donna decided to braid her hair in cornrows during "Crazy Hair" day for the school's spirit week to show support for the football team, an African American teacher confronted her by saying, "You've crossed the line." Even though the students thought it was funny and cool, the teacher perceived it as a sign of mockery of a hairstyle that is popular among Black people, rather than as a sign of school spirit. Or when the mother of one of her students was killed in a fire, Donna offered to help by taking the younger brother to the barber shop, as well as shopping for a new suit. At the funeral services, another African American teacher approached her and said, "We don't cut our kids' hair that way." Not sure of what to make of these comments at the time, Donna's explanation to me for both teachers' dissention was not only that Donna is a very effective and strong teacher but also that her students actually *like* her as a person and as a teacher. She further believes that her ability to relate to her students' lives outside school allows her to feel more connected to their community.

There are other factors (besides race) that possibly influence gay and lesbian teachers' decisions to come out or not. I asked Donna what else she thought contributed to her lack of disclosure. Just as Deneen feared other people's reaction and treatment toward her and her nephew in particular, Donna also mentioned other people's fears and their treatment of her as a White, gay woman in an urban setting. The uncertainty and misconceptions that the staff and students might have about her was too big of a battle to fight. She admits to feeling guilty because she also recognizes the need for positive, diverse role models, including gays and lesbians. Adding that the adults who are out in her building "are so extreme" suggests that this is a negative or stereotypical perception that Donna does not want to be associated with.

In addition to the issue of race and other people's homophobia, Donna also did not want to be seen as the token lesbian. Talburt (2000) asserts that as a representative of the lesbian community, there is a list of demands, "including acting true to type" (p. 57) (see entry in the Annotated Bibliography of this book). This is a requirement that Donna is not ready or willing to fulfill either. The construction of Donna's heteronormative identity certainly perpetuates heterosexism and homophobia in a school that Donna recognizes as rich in culture, yet weak in antioppressive pedagogy, especially for those with nonnormative sexual identities.

Discussion

The decision to come out in the workplace, to families, and to friends is never an easy one. Agreeing with Talburt (2000), I believe that coming out is "not a simple either/or dichotomy but a highly idiosyncratic act made in the context of social and academic knowledge, as well as in intellectual, political, and personal commitments" (p. 71). Multicultural educators who are trying to prepare students to become participants in a democracy have to begin realizing the impact on students, both academically and socially, when choosing to let others construct false identities. In my own attempts to come out, it has become clear to me that who we are racially, sexually, culturally, linguistically, economically, academically, and so on affects almost every aspect of our lives. The decisions that these teachers and I have made regarding race and sexuality were made because we felt it was the best decision at the time. It seems that all of us were trying to prevent students from getting the wrong idea about what it means to have a gay or lesbian teacher. How would they honestly feel about us as teachers? Would they still like and respect us? Would they go home and tell their families that their teacher is queer? What would happen next? How necessary is it to be out in the elementary classroom, in particular? How do we negotiate multiple identities when one of them creates a level of angst that could cost someone his or her job?

I have spoken to the three teachers several times since this inquiry first began. They are still teaching in urban schools and still hold the same beliefs regarding their decision to remain closeted. Donna has recently given birth to her second child, conceived through artificial insemination. Pregnancy, typically associated with straight women, in her case has created even more confusion for those staff members who were already questioning her sexuality. Deneen continues to be supportive of gay communities outside school, but still anticipates a backlash from staff and parents if she were to come out. Finally, Tonya, the kindergarten teacher, continues to support school policies concerning GLBT teachers and students, while also remaining active in her own professional development. However, she still refuses to disclose or discuss her sexuality, because of her professional aspiration of becoming the teachers' union president.

The confidence each of them brings to the classroom is unquestionable. However, the beliefs each holds about the intersection of race and sexuality create a tension that forces all of them to choose one form of oppression over another. Again, my work is not to explore the (lack of) validity of their claims, but rather to present their perceptions and beliefs about what it means to be gay, closeted, and a teacher in urban schools where the majority of the student population is African American and homophobia exhibits itself in much the same way as it does in the dominant White culture. One thing remains certain, regardless of community, family or workplace—the fact is that "homophobia is ingrained in our psyches through myth and media, church and state, politics and perception, and it is created and re-created within every system of public discourse" (Rhue & Rhue, 1997, p. 119).

The confluence of race and sexuality is difficult, if not impossible, to separate. I am a woman of color who is gay and I chose to stay "in" during my own teaching career. In retrospect I believe I was trying not to allow the intersection of race and sexuality to determine how others saw me. Of course I now realize that I will never have control over other people's perceptions. In addition, I think my own internalized homophobia contributed to my reluctance to come out; however, I firmly believe that "the story of one's quest to become a teacher is embedded in the story of one's life" (Bullough & Baughman, 1997). As such, I have tried to use this opportunity to share my story and the stories of Tonya, Deneen, and Donna in hopes of presenting a perspective that is respected and acknowledged as an acceptable way of being. These stories may not necessarily provide solutions or answers; that was not the goal of this inquiry. However, they may resonate with the reader in ways not thought about before. There will continue to be disagreement within the educational community, as well as in the rest of society, about the relevance of sexuality in the classroom, especially concerning the disclosure of the non-normative sexual identities of teachers. The decision to come out (or not) remains a personal decision that is undoubtedly influenced by other marginalized identities, especially race. Navigating this journey between race and sexuality may be difficult, but it certainly has a place in education.

References

Agee, J. (2004). Negotiating a teaching identity: An African American teacher's struggle to teach in test-driven contexts. *Teachers College Record 106*(4), 747–774.

Bullough, R. V., Jr., & Baughman, K. (1997). *First year teacher, 8 years later: An inquiry into teacher development*. New York: Teachers College Press.

Clandinin, D. J., & Connelly, F. M. (1994). Personal experience methods. In N. K. Norman & Y. S. Lincoln (Eds.), *Handbook of qualitative research* (pp. 413–427). Thousand Oaks, CA: Sage.

Clarke, C. (1999). The failure to transform: Homophobia in the black community. In E. Brandt (Ed.), *Dangerous liaisons: Blacks, gays, and the struggle for equality* (pp. 31–44). New York: The New York Press.

Cochran-Smith, M. (2004). *Walking the road: Race, diversity, and social justice in teacher education*. New York: Teachers College Press.

Delgado, R. (1989). Storytelling for oppositionists and others: A plea for narrative. *Michigan Law Review, 87*, 2411–2441.

Doyle, W. (1997). Heard any really good stories lately? A critique of the critics of narrative in educational research. *Teaching and Teacher Education, 13*(1), 93–99.

Du Bois, W. E. B. (1903). *The souls of Black folk*. Chicago: A.C. McClurg.

hooks, b. (1989). Homophobia in black communities. In *Talking back: Thinking feminist, thinking Black*. Boston: South End Press.

Kumashiro, K. (2001). Queer students of color and antiracist antiheterosexist education: Paradoxes of identity and activism. In K. Kumashiro (Ed.), *Troubling intersections of race and sexuality* (pp. 1–25). Lanham, MD: Rowman & Littlefield.

Ladson-Billings, G. J. (1999). Preparing teachers for diverse student populations: A critical race theory perspective. In A. Iran-Nejad & P. D. Pearson (Eds.), *Review of Research in Education* (vol. 24, pp. 211–247). Washington, DC: American Educational Research Association.

Lorde, A. (1999). There is no hierarchy of oppressions. In E. Brandt (Ed.), *Dangerous liaisons: Blacks, gays, and the struggle for equality* (pp. 306–307). New York: The New York Press.

Matsuda, M. J. (1987). Looking to the bottom: Critical legal studies and reparations. *Harvard Civil Rights–Civil Liberties Review, 72*, 30–164.

McEwan, H. (1997). The functions of narrative and research on teaching. *Teaching and Teacher Education, 13*(1), 85–92.

O'Brien, L. M., & Schillaci, M. (2002). Why do I want to teach anyway? Utilizing autobiography in teacher education. *Teaching Education, 13*(1), 25–40.

Oguntoye, K., Schultz, D., Adams, A. V., & Obitz, M. (1992). *Showing our colors: Afro-German women speak out.* Amherst, MA: University of Massachusetts Press.

Parker, L., & Lynn, M. (2002). What's race got to do with it? Critical race theory's conflicts with and connections to qualitative research methodology and epistemology. *Qualitative Inquiry, 8*(1), 7–22.

Pharr, S. (1988). *Homophobia: A weapon of sexism.* Inverness, CA: Chardon Press.

Rhue, S., & Rhue, T. (1997). Reducing homophobia in African American communities. In J. T. Sears & W. L. Williams (Eds.), *Overcoming heterosexism and homophobia: Strategies that work* (pp. 117–130). New York: Columbia University Press.

Smith, B. (1999). Blacks and gays: Healing the great divide. In E. Brandt (Ed.), *Dangerous liaisons: Blacks, gays, and the struggle for equality* (pp. 15–24). New York: The New York Press.

Talburt, S. (2000). On not coming out; Or, Reimagining limits. In W. J. Spurlin (Ed.), *Lesbian and gay studies and the teaching of English: Positions, pedagogies, and cultural politics* (pp. 54–78). Urbana, IL: National Council of Teachers of English.

10

Learning to B/Se(e) an Activist Community

The Importance of Differences in Working for Change

MOLLIE V. BLACKBURN

THIS CHAPTER IS AN EXAMINATION of our teacher inquiry group as a whole. In it, I examine the social justice work of the Pink TIGers and consider the different ways we worked, both individually and collectively, to recognize and combat heterosexism and homophobia in the world around us and in ourselves. In particular, I chronicle my personal struggle to see the group as both activist and a community. Drawing on notes, transcripts, and documents from meetings, and on interviews and emails with group members, I look across several years of our inquiry in order to see how we engaged in action for change and the role that our differences played in our efforts.

Being an Activist Community

After one reads the preceding chapters by members of the Pink TIGers, it is easy to see us as an activist community. Through inquiry projects located in elementary and high schools, university courses, and local communities, all these authors have described their intentional actions to combat heterosexism and homophobia in the places where they work and live. Reflecting on the accomplishments of these teachers, it does not feel, to me, presumptuous to name them—to name us—as activists.

In addition to the work we have done in our own educational contexts, there is the work we did together beyond our classrooms and schools. As a group, Pink TIGers have participated in events protesting the state's constitutional amendment to ban same-sex marriage; marched in Columbus, Ohio, Pride parades; testified at the statehouse in an effort to have LGBTQ people included in the state's antibullying legislation; and initiated and hosted a screening of and panel discussion around *It's* Still *Elementary* (Chasnoff & Chen, 2007), among other things. All this work, aimed at achieving equity for LGBTQ people, is activist, to be sure.

I have come to understand that what we accomplished in and beyond our classrooms and schools was fostered in our Saturday morning meetings. Certainly Jill Smith would have started her gay-straight alliance (GSA), as she describes in Chapter 8, and Anette Melvin would have considered deeply the intersections of racial and sexual identities, as she does in Chapter 9, even if we had not come together as a group. I wonder, however, whether Lauren Kenney (author of Chapter 4) would have included LGBTQ-inclusive texts in her high school English classes without the encouragement and insights she received from the group. Surely I would have gone to Pride parades, but I am not sure that I would have gone to testify at the statehouse. Even if we would have done these things without the Pink TIGers, we would have done so without a support network. At the statehouse, for example, not only were other group members there with me—Caroline Clark, Jill, and Lauren—but so were three of Lauren's students. I don't think she could have adequately prepared them to testify had she not been out as a teacher and brought in LGBT texts and films and arranged for guest speakers from TransOhio to help her students better understand the experiences of LGBTQ people and the ways that homophobia and transphobia affected them. Lauren's efforts as a teacher prompted her students to take their own steps toward activism. Together, the members of the Pink TIGers pushed one another to be stronger activists. In Jill's words, "The TIGers give me the confidence to move forward with this work—as a group we seem pretty darn fierce in ways that I could never imagine on my own."

If We Are Activists, Then Why Can't I Always See It?

Despite all these efforts to combat homophobia and heterosexism and engage in activist work, I was not always convinced that this was what was going on. The accomplishments of individuals happened over the course of years, and the protest, parades, testifying, and screening events came few and far between. Moreover, the protest and testifying events did not enjoy the results for which we had fought; that is to say that both the constitutional amendment and the antibullying legislation that fails to name LGBTQ people passed. Even the Pride parades left me with more questions. For example, a spouse of a group member noted the overt sexuality displayed at Pride. And one of the straight allies in the group expressed surprise at Pride being more of a party than a protest. Although the observations made were understandable—I probably thought something like them during my first Pride, years before—in this situation, I felt obligated to explain, if not defend, a large, diverse community of LGBTQ people to straight allies, who, while eager, still had a lot to learn.

I also experienced frustration with our monthly meetings. During our 1st year, we spent a lot of time trying to recognize homophobia and heterosexism in our classrooms and schools. We talked extensively about what homophobia and heterosexism looked like in our colleagues and students, enacted through verbal taunts we heard in our schools' hallways, such as "That's so gay!" to disapproval from our colleagues when we spoke about a new gay-themed text we were planning to use in our teaching. We talked about how it felt to encounter and combat these forms of oppression in those around us. Yet I worried about our apparent failure to recognize homophobia and heterosexism in ourselves.

These Saturday meetings, and the activist efforts of the Pink TIGers in general, stood in stark contrast to the antihomophobia work I had done earlier in my career. That work, started in 1998, had all been among LGBTQ people. At the time, I had been out as a lesbian for only a year and located my efforts in a youth-run center for LGBTQ youth. Most of the adults and even some of the youth in the center had been out as LGBT and antihomophobia activists for years. I had a lot to learn. I was not as practiced at recognizing and responding to homophobia and had not had as long in my life to experience the sting of heterosexism. The subtleties escaped me. As in these early meetings of the Pink TIGers, I probably spent a lot of time trying to recognize, to process my feelings around, and to figure out how to fight against homophobia and heterosexism in others and not seeing them in myself.

While I could recognize these differences in experiences and opportunities to process and understand how to combat homophobia and heterosexism among my Pink TIGer peers, I was still frustrated by the seeming lack of awareness and understanding exhibited by many straight ally members of the group. In this teacher inquiry group, only Jim had more experience being out as gay or lesbian and an activist for LGBT equity than I. Lauren and I had had a comparable number of years being out, but Anette was newer to being out, and everyone else was a straight ally. As allies, people were at very different places in terms of recognizing and responding to homophobia, but their experiences feeling the sting of heterosexism were, understandably, very limited. Most did not recognize times when they privileged and normalized heterosexual relationships, identities, or values over those of gay and lesbian people—including members of the Pink TIGers. This was evident in the ease with which people would say they were missing meetings for weddings, for example, a comment that cut right through me, as a person who had been in a long-term committed relationship with someone with whom I was raising a child but was denied vehemently, both historically and presently, both nationally and locally, the right to marry. This kind of comment probably would not have been said in the communities in which I previously worked, and if it had been said, it would never have gone unnoticed and uncommented on. Now, it seemed it was my responsibility to notice and comment. Noticing was not a problem for me, but commenting was. I worried that I would say something in a way that would push allies away. For a long time I did not say anything. I seemed to be paralyzed by not knowing what to do in this community that was different from the solely LGBTQ activist groups of which I had previously been a part. I had questions about whether I, as a lesbian, could work effectively with straight allies to combat homophobia and heterosexism.

The Possibilities and Limitations of Community

Not only did I struggle with seeing the community as activist, I had trouble seeing myself as activist within this community. I began to wonder whether we were a community at all, whether we should even strive to be, and whether it was even *possible* for a group like ours to be a community. I turned to scholarship to help me better understand the possibilities and limitations of communities.

I found great relief in Esterberg's (1997) claim, drawn from her study of lesbian and bisexual women's identities, that a community does not, necessarily, "share a common vision and grand agenda" (p. 176). I interpreted this to mean that what each of us imagines as the ideal outcome for our efforts—or vision—as well as the moves to make in striving for that ideal, or agenda, is different because each of us must draw on our unique experiences in the world as we imagine. These experiences include but are not limited to the students we have taught, the schools in which we have worked, and the ways we have encountered heterosexual privileges. We can complement our experiences by reading about and listening to the experiences of others, but our understandings of even others' experiences are grounded in our own. For example, we may all generically share the commitment to combating homophobia and heterosexism in classrooms and schools, but what that looks like, or what our visions for that are, may vary dramatically. Alternative imaginings are limitless. We will likely never agree on which imaginings are the right ones, as if such a thing exists. Certainly, my vision and agenda change over time. Giving up on the idea of a "common vision and grand agenda" allowed me to give up the idea that others' lives needed to align with my vision. It left me wondering, though, if we were not working toward the same vision, what was it we were working toward?

Esterberg (1997) argues that members of activist communities must work together across differences toward some action rather than toward some vision. With this argument, Esterberg posed two challenges to me. One was to search for action. Were we working together toward some action? If so, what was the action? The other was to value that our group comprised lesbians; a gay man; and allies, both male and female, because it meant we had to work across differences, something I write about in detail elsewhere (see, e.g., Blackburn, 2008) but is apparent in this chapter as well. The focus of this chapter, though, is my coming to understand our articulated commitment as more about action than vision. I examined the data representing the group—our meeting notes, transcripts of our meetings, and documents shared at our meetings—looking for action. I followed my examination with interviews with group members and email interactions over the drafts of my writing. Thus, I learned to see action in our teacher inquiry group.

Learning to See Action

Analyzing and discussing the data that document the meetings of the Pink TIGers across the years allowed me to begin to see action in our inquiry group. Consider this metaphor: It's like a film. In the meetings, it is as if I am on the set, unable to see the life of the story line. But, when I look at a single transcript, individual images cohere, as though on a movie scene, and the movement becomes evident. Then, when I look across the data, I get a sense of the whole, albeit incomplete and in process. This further helps me to see action. The metaphor, of course, falls apart. To see the whole, I would have to be a part of the daily life of each group member, in between meetings. Still, my analysis of our data reveals three ways in which we work together as an activist community: rehearsing, transcending threat, and taking tentative stances. I discuss each of these next.

Rehearsals of Possible Action

One of the things Pink TIGers do consistently in our monthly meetings and interactions is to pose dilemmas to one another, get support from one another, consider together the dynamics at play in the dilemma, and rehearse possible responses. In this way, we prepare ourselves and help prepare one another for the action we want to take in our classrooms, schools, and beyond. For example, at a meeting in December 2005, I explained to the group that Jim and I received an email in response to an article that we had coauthored (Blackburn & Buckley, 2005) on teaching queer-inclusive English language arts, and I perceived the email as homophobic. I solicited support and suggestions for response from the group.

I began by saying, "I wanted to share something that Jim and I received in response to an article that we wrote as a way of thinking about how to respond to homophobes." I distributed copies of the article, the email, and a draft of a response to the email. In this way I posed the dilemma of whether to respond to a homophobic response to my scholarship, and if so, how.

Immediately Dana, a longtime Pink TIGer, English teacher, and GSA advisor at her school, offered support by affirming my interpretation of the email author's homophobia. She said, "She starts out so evil." Caroline critiqued the emailer for trying to stay relatively anonymous by failing to name whom and where she taught. Anette and Jill expressed their frustration with the emailer's ignorance. In these ways, group members conveyed that they supported me in this dilemma. In short, they told me that they were on my side.

Although their support was valuable in and of itself, it served the more important purpose of being a foundation on which to contemplate the dynamics at play and imagine and rehearse possible further action. Caroline considered whether the emailer had even read the article. She explained that "this person could have . . . just type[d] in 'gay' and 'literature' and f[ound] anybody who's written an article and sen[t] off an email without even reading the stuff, 'I hate it, get it out of your journal.'" Dana offered evidence for Caroline's claim by pointing out that the emailer "doesn't even reference anything from the reading." Through our discussion we came to consider at least the possibility that the emailer was not critiquing the article as much as the mere idea of bringing queer themes and English language arts curricula together in schools. In other words, the email was more likely a homophobic reaction than a scholarly critique. Thus, the group helped me to understand the emailer's response as her problem of homophobia that had affected me, rather than some problem in the article itself, or with me or Jim as the authors.

Next, Jason Gonzales brought us back to the rehearsal of possible responses to the homophobia in the email. He said, "You know I'm thinking about part of a reply," so we turned to the draft of a response that I had distributed. Jim and Dana talked about how it was good to connect to the emailer's identity as a parent by mentioning my child and Jim's grandchildren. Jill said the paragraph in my draft response letter "about everyone having an agenda, I think is the strongest thing," but Lauren said she wondered whether the emailer, in Lauren's words, "has the capacity to understand that, I mean to say one person who doesn't agree with her has an agenda, do you think that she could understand that she does have an agenda?" In response, I explained, "There was an earlier version which named her agenda, but I deleted that." Jeane Copenhaver-Johnson even considered whether the "editors would be interested in publishing these, this correspondence." I then explained that I had contacted the editor to see how he would feel about my responding to the emailer, and he had said that it was fine to respond, but that she did not deserve a response. With this in mind, I did not think he would have been interested in publishing the correspondence.

Thus, the group identified passages from my draft response letter to keep and others to revise. Moreover, we considered both public and private responses. In this way, we worked together to rehearse possible responses to the homophobia we encountered. Although this conversation focused on Jim's and my encounter with homophobia, our sharing of a dilemma, solicitation and offering of support, thinking through the dilemma, and rehearsal of responses served as practice for all of our encounters with this form of hatred.

Transcendence of Threat

Another task that we have been required to do across the years, and that we have done with varying degrees of success, is to acknowledge, accept, and work within tension. Tension in the group results from group members feeling threatened. Threat, according to Fecho (2001), is inevitable in critical inquiry communities such as the Pink TIGers. He argues that threat should not be avoided or suppressed; rather, it should be experienced, worked through, and ultimately transcended. Fecho claims that this is where "meaning making seems to flourish," that is, "in zones where the current sense of self might feel threatened" (p. 13). The data representing our teacher inquiry group support this finding.

Take, for example, one of our early meetings, in the fall of 2004. We met at Anette's home, and we watched *It's Elementary* (Cohen & Chasnoff, 1997) (see entry in the Annotated Bibliography of this book). Jim, Jill, Lauren, Anette, and I were present. Among the five of us, two were university faculty (Jim and me); one was a former elementary teacher and current doctoral student (Anette); and two of us were current high school teachers (Jill and Lauren), one of whom was also a doctoral student (Jill). Although four out of the five of us self-identified as gay or lesbian, only Lauren was both lesbian (or gay) and teaching in a K–12 classroom. So, when Anette asked, in response to the film, whether it was important for teachers to be out in their classrooms and schools, it was not surprising that Lauren responded. Not only was she the only gay or lesbian person in the group who was currently in a K–12 classroom, she had also made the decision to be out as a lesbian in her classroom and school, as she describes in her chapter of this book. So, Anette said, "Why do I need to come out? Do you know what I mean? Why, when, is it relevant? If I teach gay curriculum, is it relevant for me to come out?" Lauren answered immediately:

> Well, what I feel like is, the reason I came out is because in high
> school for me, I didn't have any out gay teachers, but I know
> that I had gay teachers, like my English teacher and my chemis-
> try teacher lived together for 25 years. . . . But they never talked
> about it. . . . So I thought as a young person that it's okay to be gay,
> like, I like both of them and they are okay. It's okay to be gay if
> you don't talk about it because it might gross some people out or
> whatever. And my teachers who were straight, who were just get-
> ting married or had been married for a while, would just be like,

"Oh, yeah, my husband is a chemist and he knows about that,"
or whatever. They would mention it in class or they would have
their wedding bands on or whatever, so it was like, oh it's okay
to talk about it if you're married, but not if you're gay. And so for
me, what I wanted to do when I was a teacher, when I was starting
teaching, I wanted to come out because I wanted them to see that
I'm not ashamed. I'm a gay person who cares about them, who
is not preying on them, and this is what it looks like and I'm not
going to tell you about having sex and I'm not going to talk about
whatever. But I am going to tell you that my partner is a writer
and this applied because whatever. And it's just like a part of who
I am, you can ask me questions, I'm not embarrassed or anything
like that. And if you are gay, it's okay. And so I wanted to be like
an example and for me that was important. That's why I felt like it
was relevant.

Anette, who was no longer a K–12 teacher, and who had not come out
at her school when she was, suggested that coming out for her would
be a different undertaking from Lauren's because Lauren is White and
Anette is biracial, which, in her words, "is considered Black in this country." Anette pointed to the significance of her race in her teaching by telling us that she was one of only two teachers of color in her school and that
an administrator had asked her to correct the district's notation of her race
from White to Black. Later she said:

Basically, I felt that trying to be a role model for all the kids in that
building, especially all the biracial and Black kids, was more important because race was an issue in our building, for Black and
White students.

In other words, when and where she was teaching, she experienced race
as a more important issue for her to address than sexuality.

Anette then shifted the focus from teachers being out to including
LGBTQ themes in their curricula. Later she explained to me that she was
thinking, "'Why is this relevant to teaching 2nd graders?'" She asked specifically about including LGBTQ themes in curricula that are already too
full with testing preparations. She asked, "So how do you incorporate it
into your regular curriculum when you have all these other pressures and
accountability to raise your test scores?" Again, Lauren responded. She

explained that because her school allocated time for test preparation and because her students had a high pass rate, there was less pressure to do this work in her regular curricula. She went on to say that she addressed questions that were posed to her as an out gay teacher in response to literature and film, and she taught "social justice stuff" with whatever skills she was teaching. She did not, however, talk explicitly about including LGBTQ themes in her curricula.

I think it is fair to say that this discussion posed varying degrees of threat for Anette and Lauren. Lauren could have understood Anette's question to be a critique of Lauren's decision to be an out teacher, and Anette could have interpreted Lauren's response to be a critique of Anette's decision not to be out as a K–12 teacher. In turn, Lauren could have heard Anette to be saying that as a White person, Lauren was not in a place to say what Anette should or should not do. Then, Lauren may have felt vulnerable when the discussion moved to curricula, since Lauren's curriculum was not, at that time, LGBTQ-inclusive. Given these possible understandings, to say that the discussion was a zone "where the current sense of self might feel threatened," to use Fecho's (2001, p. 13) words, seems reasonable. And like Fecho's findings on such zones being sites of meaning-making, so was this.

The meaning made from this particular discussion is evident in Anette and Lauren's chapters in this book. Anette's project was to explore what race has to do with gay and lesbian teachers being out (or not) in their classrooms and schools. Lauren's project was to consider the impact of her being out, but also to include LGBTQ themes deliberately and explicitly in her curricula, keeping in mind the role of testing on her efforts. Moreover, her analysis shows her reflection on what race has to do with being out at school, particularly with respect to her students. Thus, this discussion, which I would characterize as tense, even threatening at times, provoked significant and productive intellectual and activist work.

Taking Tentative Stances

A third way that our teacher inquiry community functions in activist ways is by fostering, if not demanding, opportunities for group members to claim tentative stances. At monthly meetings, group members must consciously take stands on issues, knowing that our positions may change as we hear more perspectives, consider other aspects of issues, and have different experiences in our lives. Group members must also hear one another with the knowledge that others may change their positions as well. In other words, all of us must be invited to take a strong stand on an issue but then be supported in our efforts to shift our stances or change our philosophical locations relative to that issue. In this way, individual members of the Pink TIGers, and the group as a whole, progress over time. This progress gets taken up in evolving actions, as the account below shows.

Before the group began meeting, in the spring of 2004, Dana was asked by students to help start and to serve as advisor to the GSA at her school. The students hoped to initiate the GSA in the fall of 2004, and Dana was eager to support them in their efforts. She was, however, discouraged by several colleagues, her faculty mentor at the school, one of her school's administrators, and a parent of one her students, all of whom were concerned about the controversy that might arise from forming a GSA at the school and the effects this might have on Dana, both personally and professionally. School administrators suggested that she start a cultural diversity club in lieu of a GSA, and Dana agreed to their suggestion. In our second Pink TIGer meeting, in September 2004, Dana described to us what she explained to the resistant parent: "If we're doing cultural diversity, because [the LGBTQ community] is a subculture in our society, then we're doing cultural diversity, everything, I'm talking about everything." Moreover, to us, she characterized the club as an "underground version" of a GSA. At this point, her stance toward her extracurricular efforts at combating homophobia was that this work could be accomplished through a cultural diversity club. Her stance was based on the belief that LGBTQ people would be included in a cultural diversity club and the notion that the club would be intended to serve as a GSA in a surreptitious way. This stance was fortified by her determination to make such LGBTQ social justice work happen despite the barriers she faced—to fight homophobia through the cultural diversity club. Jill talked about how she was also asked to name her GSA something more ambiguous but that she refused, suggesting her disagreement with Dana's stance.

Six months later, at another TIGer meeting, Dana talked about how much more her group was able to accomplish under the name of *cultural diversity* than it could have with the name "gay-straight alliance." She said, "I'll stick myself under a rock and call it a different name. I don't care because so much has gotten accomplished." As such, it seemed that her previous stance was again reinforced.

Two things happened at that meeting, though, that seemed to challenge her stance. One was her report of a homophobic hate crime that was committed between students who attended her school. Several students had written "fag" and left a dead cat on another student's car. Immediately after hearing about this crime, Dana assumed the role of what she later came to recognize as a GSA advisor. In her words, she "emailed his [the victim's] family, talked with administration, discussed what to do with [Mollie], and became an overall advocate for that student." The school claimed no responsibility, since the crime took place off school grounds and outside school hours. I suggested that the school's response to this incident was not surprising, considering how the school had evaded an opportunity to support LGBTQ people by proposing a cultural diversity club instead of a GSA. This connection raised the question of how a GSA, as opposed to a cultural diversity club, may have responded to this event.

The second thing that happened was that two young men stopped by and joined the group's meeting for a little while. One of the two was Dana's former student. The other had been the victim of a homophobic hate crime the previous night, which was evident in his injured face. Dana explained to us that her student had been "dying to come and visit" the TIGers and explained to the other young man, "[You] are in the best place. We'll all support and love you." Their coming to our meeting that day suggested to me that a teacher inquiry group committed to combating homophobia in schools was a more suitable alternative to a GSA than a cultural diversity club was, at least for these young people. At this point, Dana later shared her feelings with me about accepting a cultural diversity club in lieu of a GSA and that she "really felt like a fool, someone who believed that everything was going to be okay, but then it wasn't."

It was a year later, in April 2006, when Dana acknowledged that LGBTQ students did not participate in the cultural diversity club. Caroline asked, "Do the kids who would populate the GSA belong to the diversity club?" Dana responded: "They don't; they're separate from that, and that's the big frustration. And they're, like, why don't you, it's not helping me, that's not what [another student in the school] wants; [he] wants a GSA." Moreover, eventually Dana stated that the students who did come to the cultural diversity club were not interested in prioritizing LGBTQ-ally work. In other words, she came to recognize the limits of the cultural diversity club, at least as it took shape in her school, in combating homophobia.

Around this time, her students again asked her to help them start a GSA. At this point she was a very active member of our teacher inquiry group. As she described it,

It was my involvement in the group that really motivated me. Actually as I learned about our goals and became really attuned to why I was there (as an individual), then my overall fear of losing everything was ignored. Because of the group, I wanted to be the activist we talked about each month. I don't want to sound all "I did it for the group," but I was motivated by the voices in the group—Jill's struggles, Annette's choices, Lauren's experiences, and also to really support your reason for inviting me into the group. . . . Simply stated, the group motivated me. It still does.

Given her motivation and commitment, she was determined to make the GSA happen for her students. And given her prior experiences, she was prepared for the resistance she might encounter from her administrators. In an appointment with her building administrator, she came armed with a list of local schools that had GSAs; the names of their advisors and building principals; and a letter of support from me, as a university representative. She also came having learned more from the Gay, Lesbian, and Straight Education Network's (GLSEN) website about how to start a GSA and having learned more about what the local queer youth center could and could not provide for her students. It was during this time, Dana later told me, that she "learned that [her] knowledge was more powerful than their rules and threats." Being so prepared paid off. Her school permitted her to serve as the advisor for students who have initiated and facilitated a GSA at her high school. The GSA became an active organization within her high school. Moreover, it has a vibrant life outside the school in that members come to regular book discussion groups at the local LGBTQ youth center and have connected with neighboring schools to help other young people start their own GSAs.

Over the years, Dana's stance changed from understanding the cultural diversity club as a place, perhaps the only place, that could accomplish antihomophobia work in her school while addressing a wide array of cultural issues; to wondering whether this club could accomplish all of this work; to insisting that her school needed a GSA in order to address homophobia directly. I am not saying that Dana was wrong and came to be right. I would suggest that there were many variables that made her earlier stance make the most sense in that time and place, relative to the school, Dana, and her students, and that there were just as many variables that made her later stance make the most sense then and there, given changes in the school, Dana, and her students. I am arguing instead that by *taking tentative stances*, Dana could implement an action, evaluate its impact, consider alternative actions, then implement those, and so forth and so on. She later explained to me that it was through this process that, in addition to starting the GSA, she came to remember her "goals as an advocate and that [she] can not be afraid to 'speak out' for what [she] believe[s] in." Her advocacy and clear stance as a straight ally have resulted in students in her GSA coming to her to discuss issues in their lives and potential ways of handling them, as well as in LGBTQ students who have never attended her GSA but who know her to be the advisor coming to her for advice. As such, she now serves as a resource and advocate for a wide array of students in her school. Thus, Dana's experiences offer an illustration of how the potential for social change lies in the taking of tentative stances and their related actions and reflections.

An Activist Community

I understand our rehearsal, transcendence of threat, and tentative stances as they take shape in our Saturday morning meetings as actions, albeit small actions, but imperative ones that lay the groundwork for the more substantial activist work we have done beyond our monthly meetings. These actions, both small and large, convince me that our community is an activist one and that each of us is a more powerful activist as a result of our regular and extended participation in this teacher inquiry group. In fact, Trimbur (1989) argues, "It is through the social interaction of shared activity that individuals realize their own power to take control of their situation by collaborating with others" (p. 604). This is what I see in the Pink TIGers from studying the data representing our collective inquiry: I see all of us be(com)ing activists.

Early in this chapter, I expressed my frustration with the group based on my fear that we would not be an activist community in part because of our diversity, especially in terms of our sexual identities. I started with this frustration in part because it is the story of my question. It explains why I learned what I learned. A different story would have led me to a different question, different scholarship, different analyses, findings, and implications. But this story, my story, led me here. I worried that the lesbians and gay man would have to go too far backward in trying to explain what homophobia and heterosexism, both overt and subtle, looked like in our lives to ever move forward. I worried that I would be made too vulnerable to group members' buried homophobia and heterosexism. I worried that my responses to such forms of oppression would be anger, and that my anger would scare away allies.

From here, though, I can see that we were not moving backward; we were moving forward. We were learning. According to Trimbur (1989), learning is "joining new communities and taking part in new conversations" (p. 605). For some of us, we were learning to see homophobia and heterosexism; for others, we were learning how to work productively with allies, among many other things. For me, learning to work with allies meant learning to believe that allies cared enough to want to hear what I had to say, even when they were implicated in what I had to say. It meant learning to trust that they could handle it. It also meant learning to say what I had to say in ways that could be heard as supportive rather than offensive, something I imagine I will struggle with my entire life. When I think about what all of us were learning, it becomes obvious to me that we were all moving forward. All of us were learning to be a part of an activist community in our activist community, and that we were able to do this was dependent on our differences. As mentioned in Chapter 1 of this book, Esterberg (1997) claims that community members must work across differences in order for the community to be what she calls a "strategy for social change" (p. 175). According to her, working across differences for "social and political actions" forces us to "stretch ourselves" (p. 176). In doing so, "we learn new tools for social and political action" (p. 176). In other words, being a group of male and females, allies, lesbians, and a gay man was our strength rather than our weakness. It was foundational to our activism.

What we did with those differences determined to what degree we built on that foundation. Trimbur (1989) advocates for "collective examinations of how people differ, where their differences come from, and whether they can live and work together with these differences" (p. 610). He claims that through such "collective investigation(s) of differences, [participants] can begin to imagine ways to change the relations of production and to base the conversation not on consensus but on reciprocity and the mutual recognition of the participants and their differences" (p. 614). In doing this work, participants are better able "to imagine alternative worlds and transformations of social life and labor" (p. 615). Similarly, when the Pink TIGers were able to recognize, understand, and respect our differences, we were better equipped to accomplish our activist work.

That our differences and our work across them provoked us to be more powerful activists brings me back to the more important reason for my beginning this chapter with my frustration. My frustration represents the frustration inherent in working across differences. This chapter could have just as easily been framed in Lauren's frustration with Anette's failure to value the work she was doing by being an out lesbian teacher, or Anette's frustration with Lauren for failing to recognize the role of race in choosing to be out (or not) as a teacher. I wrote about my own frustration because I know it most intimately; but all of us, as we worked across differences, experienced frustration. Frustration can be an obstacle to our work, to be sure. It can hinder our progress. It can terminate our progress by serving as a catalyst for choosing to prioritize other work, easier work. That the people in this book, as well as members of the Pink TIGers who elected not to write, refused to allow their frustrations to push them away from the very difficult work of combating homophobia and heterosexism in classrooms and schools is remarkable. It reveals the strength of these people, the force of the group. It reveals our commitments and passions. The strength, force, commitments, and passions bring us together, again and again, despite the frustrations.

If this is the kind of work you want to do, I encourage you to put your commitments and passions out in the world for others to see. Some will be repelled, but others will be drawn to your values, not because they mirror their own, but because between you there is a promise of learning, teaching, and getting into some difficult work that matters. I encourage you to connect with those who are drawn to this promise. Among those of you drawn to the promise, love yourselves for being committed to the work. Support one another in the work. Together, rehearse possible ways of responding to heterosexism and homophobia. Challenge yourselves to listen to and understand alternative perspectives. Actively seek such perspectives. Allow yourselves to experience and transcend threat. Assert strong stances, but continue to listen and learn, and respect your right, as well as the rights of others, to change where you stand. Do not allow your inevitable frustrations to thwart you. All the while, work for change in your classroom, school, and broader community. Such is the work of an activist community.

References

Blackburn, M. V. (2008, November). Community as rhizome: Rupture and lines of flight in a teacher inquiry group. In D. S. Warriner (Organizer), *The problem with "community": Rethinking participation, contestation, and imagination in spaces of teaching and learning.* Paper presented at the annual meeting of the American Anthropological Association, San Francisco.

Blackburn, M. V., & Buckley, J. F. (2005). Teaching queer-inclusive English language arts. *Journal of Adolescent and Adult Literacy, 49*(3), 202–212.

Chasnoff, D. (Producer & Director), & Chen, S. (Producer). (2007). *It's* still *elementary* [Motion picture]. (Available from Groundspark, San Francisco, CA.)

Cohen, H. S. (Producer), & Chasnoff, D. (Producer & Director). (1997). *It's elementary: Talking about gay issues in school* [Motion picture]. (Available from Women's Educational Media, San Francisco, CA.)

Esterberg, K. G. (1997). *Lesbian and bisexual identities: Constructing communities, constructing selves.* Philadelphia: Temple University Press.

Fecho, B. (2001). "Why are you doing this?": Acknowledging and transcending threat in a critical inquiry classroom. *Research in the Teaching of English, 36*(1), 9–37.

Trimbur, J. (1989). Consensus and difference in collaborative learning. *College English, 51*(6), 602–616.

11

Acting Out!
So What?

CAROLINE T. CLARK, MOLLIE V. BLACKBURN,
LAUREN M. KENNEY, AND JILL M. SMITH

I N THINKING ABOUT THE END OF OUR BOOK, it is worth reflecting on the beginning of it, our title: *Acting Out!*

Acting Out!

We use this exhortation intentionally and with varied meaning. Most obviously, it takes up the idea of being "out." For Pink TIGers like Lauren,
Anette, and Mollie, this has meant coming out and being out as lesbian,
as well as making choices, shaped in part by sociocultural and institutional contexts, around when to be out, or not, and the risks and advan-
tages involved in these choices. For Lauren, being out, and studying the
effects of this choice on her students, colleagues, and school community,
are central to her inquiry work as a teacher. Even in her school, with a
supportive administration, her choice evoked potential and real threats
to herself and her students, such as the homophobic parent who withdrew his daughter from the school because he did not want his child to
have a lesbian teacher. Alternatively, for Anette, the choice to stay "in"
in the classroom, and to understand this choice through the lens of race,
has shaped how she currently works, as an out lesbian of color, in her
research with lesbian teachers in urban schools trying to understand the
risks they feel about being out, or not, in their classrooms and communities. For Mollie, working as an out lesbian activist with LGBTQ youth

shaped her views of activism, a view that, initially, did not fit neatly with the work of the Pink TIGers. Through her inquiry work, she came to work through her frustrations and see the group as an activist community, one that, through our differences, was better equipped to combat heterosexism and homophobia in one another and in the wider world by addressing and transcending threat (Fecho, 2001).

For Pink TIGers like Jason, Mindy, Jill, Ryan, Ariel, Jeane, and Caroline, "out" has meant coming out and being out as allies—straight people who advocate for LGBTQ rights and fight against homophobia and heterosexism. Here, too, sociocultural and institutional contexts and their influence on these educators' choices have shaped the nature of their being out. As out allies in schools, Mindy, Jason, and Jill encountered degrees of threat and risk, from the risks that Mindy took to turn "teachable moments" into fuller opportunities to address homophobia and heterosexism in her elementary teaching, to the not-so-subtle threats implied by Jason's colleagues when he chose to teach the gay-themed short story "A Letter to Harvey Milk" (Newman, 1988; see entry in the Annotated Bibliography of this book), to the near loss of her long-held job teaching high school English when Jill worked to start and sustain a GSA in her suburban school. For novice teachers Ryan and Ariel, the risks of running a GSA as 1st-year teachers was overcome, in part, by their inquiry work to learn about the community; their recognition of the importance of balance; and their capacity to create support systems for themselves by building relationships of trust with colleagues, families, students, and community groups, including their decision to join the Pink TIGers and work on these issues through focused teacher inquiry. While Jeane and Caroline were out as allies in the relatively safer confines of their university settings, both encountered student resistance and, in some ways, enacted their own resistance to truly challenging homophobia and heterosexism in their students.

In addition to focusing attention on being out, our title calls attention to action. Our inquiry projects, detailed in individual chapters, show how members of the Pink TIGers have worked as activists in our own classrooms and schools. Lauren, for example, found that being out was not enough to combat homophobia and heterosexism in her school. Starting a GSA and using queer-inclusive literature in her classroom provided opportunities for her to take on homophobia and, eventually, transphobia among her students in active ways. Mindy, through her work as a teacher and multicultural coordinator in her district, has been able to make her out-ally status a visible part of her work to address sexuality as part of diversity with teachers and students in her community. And Jill, through her careful self-reflection and analysis, traces the shifts in her own development as an ally, documenting her setbacks, silence, and eventual empowerment and action to change school policy to be more explicitly supportive of LGBTQ students and colleagues.

As a group, too, we have acted out. Mollie's chapter documents our collective activist work. Some of this action occurred in the community, like protesting the state's constitutional amendment to ban same-sex marriage; marching in Columbus, Ohio, Pride parades; testifying at the statehouse in an effort to have LGBTQ people included in the state's antibullying legislation; and initiating and hosting a public screening of *It's Elementary* and *It's Still Elementary* (Cohen & Chasnoff, 1996; Chasnoff & Chen, 2007; see entries in the Annotated Bibliography in this book). Our decision to host this screening was a result of having watched, discussed, and been affected by the earlier documentary. Moreover, we complemented the screening with a panel discussion of our efforts to combat homophobia in schools. Thus, our regular discussions of films at our monthly TIGer meetings prompted us to act out in more public ways. But as Mollie's analysis shows, much of the group's action occurred more slowly and prosaically in our teacher inquiry meetings, where members rehearsed possible action, worked to transcend threat by holding one another accountable for our own enactments of homophobia and heterosexism, and took tentative stances that were open to challenge and potential revision through our discussions and subsequent reflection.

At monthly meetings, Lauren, Jason, Mindy, Jill, Ryan, and Ariel helped us understand, firsthand, what heterosexism and homophobia look like in local schools and classrooms, and approaches they took to combating these forces. For example, they shared how LGBT-themed texts and films were received (or resisted) by students in their English teaching, prompting other members to adopt similar texts or adapt lessons to avoid potential conflict. An example was when Lauren discussed her successful screening of the film *Ma Vie en Rose*, and Jill was prompted to use the same film at one of her GSA's subsequent meetings. Anette, Mollie, Jeane, and Caroline listened and learned from their stories, using these accounts to illustrate for their university students, both pre- and in-service teachers as well as those preparing to be teacher educators and educational researchers, the real risks, as well as rewards, of working against heterosexism and homophobia in schools. For instance, because of Ryan and Ariel's work coadvising the GSA, Caroline was able to share stories of their experiences with her preservice teachers, providing a concrete example that it is, in fact, possible to work for social justice and be a straight ally in public schools even in one's 1st year on the job. Through her individual inquiry, exploring the intersections of race and sexuality and their effects on teacher identity, Anette pushed all of us to consider how race and racism affected our commitments to combating heterosexism and homophobia and to see color (and, at times, the absence of color) in discussions of LGBT rights. Diane Finnerty's essay, "An Open Letter to My White Lesbian, Gay, Bisexual, Transgender Sisters and Brothers" (see entry in the Annotated Bibliography of this book), became a touchstone text, changing not only the way we talked together about race, sexuality, and privilege, but also the way we worked to act in the world on these issues. And Ryan and Ariel, through their experiences with their community's gay-straight-Christian alliance, along with shared readings like the pamphlet *The Bible Is an Empty Closet* (Blair, 2009) and the *Essence* article "All God's Children" (Reeves, 1999) (see entries in the Annotated Bibliography of this book), helped us to consider and reconsider the somewhat easy generalizations and associations we made about Christians' attitudes toward LGBT people.

A third kind of acting out emphasizes neither the being out nor the actions of Pink TIGers. Rather, this kind of acting out emphasizes the two words together: acting out, like a child expressing herself in ways that are deemed socially unacceptable. Like this child, Pink TIGers acted out by naming and examining issues deemed socially unacceptable in educational contexts because we want them, even need them, to be addressed not only for ourselves but also for the students we serve. While these temper tantrums, if you will, are not represented by our writing, the writing, and the work more generally, is at least in part fueled by these tantrums. We're thinking, in particular, of one of Jim's last meetings, before he became too ill to participate. It was in March 2006. Jim reported that a reference librarian on his campus harassed Jim based on his sexuality by recommending that all incoming freshman read a book that offers a rationale for homophobia. Jim rightly felt attacked by the librarian's suggestion, and, moreover, he felt a lack of support from his administration, faculty, and human resources representative. Jim was furious, not only at his job, but also in our meeting. There was, what we understood to be, nervous laughter from some of the group members, and Jim banged his hands on the table, demanding that we take his fury seriously. In retrospect, we understand Jim was acting out, not in a way that suggested immaturity, but in a way that revealed intensity. Both in his job and at this meeting, Jim named and examined the ways in which the librarian not only imposed his homophobia on Jim and other people on their campus but also fostered this hatred in others by trying to offer an entire incoming class of students a book that encouraged if not provoked homophobic values. He did this not because it was easy or even socially acceptable but because it needed to be done, for himself, his colleagues, and his students. In these ways the Pink TIGers have acted out against heterosexism and homophobia in schools and classrooms.

So What?

So, here we are. So this is the end of the book. So what? As JoBeth Allen (2007) writes,

> So . . . this is the action punctuated so, the one that is not a conclusion but an intrusion into our comfortable lives as researchers. It is the one that demands that we move—somewhere, do—something. So. It is the most elusive, troubling, complex, nagging, and important word in any research report. (p. 77).

The answer to Allen's question—So what?—is different for different people. Therefore, Allen provokes us to ask, and in turn answer, this question: So what difference does the kind of work the Pink TIGers do make for whom?

K–12 students who share classrooms and schools with teachers who are committed to antihomophobia work have the distinct privilege of learning in an environment that, at least in part, strives to respect diverse populations. Think of the students in Lauren's classroom who, because of her willingness to take the risk and be out in her school, were able to connect better with an open and honest teacher who was investing her energy in them rather than wasting it on closeting herself. Reflect on Mindy's students who had the opportunity to consider how being gay may be a biological trait rather than a disrespected choice and to discuss the consequences of such a possibility. In thinking about this, recall, in particular, the one student who was so drawn to this conversation that he moved, desk and all, nine feet closer to the facilitator. Consider Jason's students who were able to observe their teacher take a risk for something he believed in by reading and discussing a gay-themed text with students in class. Imagine being one of Jill's students who had the privilege of seeing his or her teacher come to understand and work within and against her own privilege as a straight, White, middle-class adult in a ceaseless effort to overcome homophobic obstacles in order to make their community a better place for all people to teach and learn. And, finally, think of Ryan and Ariel's students who witness teachers who could be understood as vulnerable as a result of their youth and newness to their careers work together and with others, even others with quite distinct commitments, for social change. For all these teachers' students, the work of the Pink TIGers matters. It benefits not only LGBTQ people who come to see themselves as valuable contributors to communities but also all people who have the chance to relinquish socially sanctioned forms of hatred and to become their most loving and powerful selves.

Pre- and in-service teachers who share courses with faculty who are committed to antihomophobia work have the unique opportunity to be prepared to create such educational opportunities for their students. Reflect on Jeane's powerful reflections on Kyle, a student resistant to her antihomophobia work. Such resistance is inevitable in the kind of work the Pink TIGers do. And think of Caroline's students, even those from years ago, who read and discussed texts about LGBTQ people in schools in her class when they weren't doing so elsewhere and ultimately those who benefit from her nuanced understanding of various stances preservice teachers tend to take when engaging this topic. Pre- and in-service teachers in classes like Jeane's and Caroline's benefit from their teachers' antihomophobia work not only because it serves as a model of teaching to make a difference but also because it is powerfully informed by their profound reflection on their efforts.

Teachers and researchers, such as those described above, who engage in antihomophobia work with an ongoing teacher inquiry group designed to support their efforts are, as Mollie captures it, challenged repeatedly to rehearse and improve responses to the heterosexism and homophobia they encounter, transcend threat among one another, and take tentative stances that allow them both to assert and contest their, indeed our, beliefs. Consider Anette's exploration of her personal history as it is informed by her race-focused interviews with lesbian teachers. Her study allowed her to rehearse arguments for being closeted as well as those for being out; thus she was able to assert multiple, variable, and even conflicting stances on the issue. In doing so, she effectively transcended threats posed in the group, as described by Mollie. Work like this teaches all of us the complexity of our efforts. As such, it holds more potential to make social change. Thus, it matters—for our students and ourselves. It holds the possibility of mattering to your students and you too.

So What Now?

The Pink TIGers are currently in their 5th year of meeting. We have lost some original members, and we have gained some new ones. We have enjoyed but have now moved through the funding we received from NCTE's Research Foundation that funded our teacher inquiry group meeting time, travel to conferences, and ultimately the reflective time and space it took for us to prepare and write this book. We expect that we will continue to meet as long as there is a substantial group committed to meeting, albeit on the cheap. We will continue to find, share, read, watch, and discuss texts that inform our efforts to combat heterosexism and homophobia in schools and classrooms. We will continue our work in and beyond our classrooms. We imagine that we have more to learn ahead of us than we can possibly know at this time, but we are ready. Ready to learn and to get better at acting out. We invite you to join us.

References

Allen, J. (2007). "So . . ." In M. V. Blackburn & C. T. Clark (Eds.), *Literacy research for political action and social change* (pp. 77–94). New York: Peter Lang.

Blair, R. (2009). *The Bible is an empty closet.* Retrieved January 8, 2009, from http://www.whosoever.org/v3i3/closet.html

Chasnoff, D. (Producer & Director) & Chen, S. (Producer). (2007). *It's* still *elementary* [Motion picture]. (Available from Groundspark, San Francisco, CA.)

Cohen, H. S. (Producer) & Chasnoff, D. (Producer & Director). (1996). *It's elementary: Talking about gay issues in school* [Motion picture]. (Available from Women's Educational Media, San Francisco, CA.)

Fecho, B. (2001). "Why are you doing this?": Acknowledging and transcending threat in a critical inquiry classroom. *Research in the Teaching of English, 36*(1), 9–37.

Finnerty, D. (2004). *An open letter to my White lesbian, gay, bisexual, transgender sisters and brothers.* Retrieved July 7, 2009, from http://www.tolerance.org/images/teach/current/Open_Letter.pdf

Newman, L. (1988). A letter to Harvey Milk. *A letter to Harvey Milk: Short stories* (pp. 25–28). Ithaca, NY: Firebrand Books.

Reeves, K. E. (1999). All God's children. *Essence, 30*(7), 220.

Annotated Bibliography

Blair, R. *The Bible is an empty closet*. Retrieved January 8, 2009, from http://www.whosoever.org/v3i3/closet.html

This brief pamphlet and website discusses the limited degree to which the Bible informs readers' understandings of homosexuality. It relies heavily on quotations of theologians and scholars of sexuality to support this argument. It examines closely scripture that is often drawn on in an effort to condemn homosexuals. Ultimately, this piece argues that the Bible has "nothing specific to say about Homosexuality" but "plenty to say about God's grace to all people and God's call to justice and mercy."

Mollie (author of Chapter 10) brought this piece, in the form of a pamphlet, to the group early in its 1st year of meeting as a way of bolstering group members' abilities to respond to attacks of their antihomophobia work as anti-Christian. Eventually we read Alex Sanchez's *God Box*, a young adult novel exploring similar tensions, which seemed to some to be more effective at preparing group members for such attacks.

Brant, B. (1991). *Food and spirits*. Ithaca, NY: Firebrand Books.

This collection of short stories is written by a Native American writer who focuses on women with the strength to endure and escape horrid violations at the hands of the men in their lives. The strength of these women is often intertwined with their familial relationships with other women.

We selected this book after reading Osborne's chapter in Spurlin's *Lesbian and Gay Studies and the Teaching of English*. (This chapter is annotated below.) It is prefaced by a poem that challenged us, as teachers writing about our activist efforts, by asking, "What good is this pen, this yellow paper, if I can't fashion them into tools or weapons to change our lives?" and reminded us that "this is not safe—being a writer" (p. 14).

Cloud, J. (2005, October 2). The battle over gay teens. *Time*. Retrieved January 8, 2009, from http://www.time.com/time/magazine/article/0,9171,1112856,00. html

> In this article, Cloud states that young people are claiming and revealing their homosexuality at an earlier age than they once did. Two gay youth organizations were featured in this article. One group, the Point Foundation, is a national organization created to help gay youth, in part by offering generous scholarships. It was created by Bruce Lindstrom after his finding few gay groups that did much for young people. The other, Exodus Youth (part of Exodus International), is a group for Christians struggling with same-sex attractions. The latter group was designed to turn homosexuals into heterosexuals.
>
> This article was a starting point for a Pink TIGers' discussion examining various perspectives on gay youth in the United States. We talked about the growing numbers of out gay teens and how this relates to the experiences group members have had with GSAs in their schools.

Chasnoff, D. (Producer & Director), & Chen, S. (Producer). (2007). *It's still elementary* [Motion picture]. (Available from Groundspark, San Francisco, CA.)

> Through revisiting the original *It's Elementary* documentary, *It's Still Elementary* explores the impact of LGBT educational activism in two educational arenas. First, the documentary looks at the public's role by telling the story of the creation and reception of *It's Elementary*, including the initial struggles in filming, controversy surrounding a PBS broadcast, and right-wing responses. Second, the film examines how antihomophobia work in schools affects students. In order to show the long-term impact of such work, these sections follow up with several people who were students in the classrooms of the first film.
>
> As a group, the Pink TIGers supported a public screening of the film and panel discussion. One major goal of this screening was to begin conversations regarding educational LGBT activist work with as many other educators, administrators, and community members as possible. A second goal was to provide resources and support for teachers choosing to be allies and do activist work. At the event, the film served as an overview of antihomophobia work in schools, while the panel discussion brought the issues back to our community, allowing attendees to ask questions that probed deeper into the ground broken by the documentary.

Cohen, H. S. (Producer), & Chasnoff, D. (Producer & Director). (1996). *It's elementary: Talking about gay issues in school* [Motion picture and guide]. (Available from Women's Educational Media, San Francisco, CA.)

While other sources demonstrate the pressing need to address homophobia and heterosexism in schools, Cohen and Chasnoff's documentary shows the possibility of discussing LGBT issues in K–8 educational settings. The film focuses on a variety of public and private K–8 schools where educators teach lessons designed to combat homophobia. Dialogue between students alongside the words of practicing educators drive the film forward, leaving viewers with a concrete picture of what age-appropriate discussions of LGBT issues look like.

As a group, the Pink TIGers have used *It's Elementary* in several ways. We have viewed and discussed the film in order to inform our own activism, specifically regarding how we discuss LGBT issues with our students. Various members have also used the documentary in their own classrooms or GSAs in order to start conversations with students regarding the many issues raised by the film. These classrooms have ranged from high school settings to teacher education programs.

DiGangi, M. (2000). Shakespeare's sexuality: Who needs it? In W. J. Spurlin (Ed.), *Lesbian and gay studies and the teaching of English: Positions, pedagogies, and cultural politics* (pp. 147–167). Urbana, IL: National Council of Teachers of English.

This chapter gives an overview of Shakespeare and how his writing has been appropriated and debated with regard to homo- and heterosexualities. This chapter begins as a response to the accusation that queer theory and pedagogy are "trendy" and somehow distract from more legitimate academic practices. In defense of including discussion of Shakespeare's sexuality, the author reviews how scholars and public figures throughout history have debated and variously appropriated Shakespeare's work as representing same-sex love or opposite-sex love.

The Pink TIGers read this piece just before Jason (author of Chapter 5) started reading and studying *Romeo and Juliet* with 9th graders. It inspired him to ask questions about the homoerotic possibilities between Romeo and Mercutio. It helped him understand that such questioning was legitimate.

Eckes, S. E., & McCarthy, M. M. (2008). GLBT teachers: The evolving legal protections. *American Educational Research Journal, 45*(3), 530–554.

This comprehensive review article examines two bodies of information relative to the rights of GLBT teachers in public schools. First, the authors analyze all litigation pertaining to GLBT educators; next, they examine the antidiscrimination employment laws of all 50 states.

The TIGers were interested in this article on many levels. First, we were interested in learning more about the legal protections in various states and having concrete information to share with LGBTQ K–12 colleagues and university preservice teachers who want to know what it will mean for them, legally, to be out in schools. Second, because of our work on state and local antibullying policies, and on doing policy work in schools, especially the work of Jill (author of Chapter 8), we were particularly interested in the authors' conclusions that work needs to occur beyond the federal and state level. They suggest that "city and school district nondiscrimination policies should be expanded to protect GLBT pubic educators and other public employees. Until societal sentiments toward GLBT teachers change substantially, these employees need laws and policies to protect them from negative employment consequences." We see this kind of policy work as part of the work of the Pink TIGers.

Evans, R. (Director & Author). (2004). *Brother to brother* [Motion picture]. (Available at www.wolfevideo.com)

This film by Rodney Evans explores the life and struggles of Perry Williams, a young Black gay artist in contemporary New York. Trying to come to terms with his sexual identity as a Black gay man, he meets an older Black gay poet who was part of the Harlem Renaissance in the 1930s. Suddenly, these two find themselves traveling back and forth in time to the likes of Langston Hughes, James Baldwin, and Zora Neale Hurston, who help Perry gain some perspective on his own life.

Anette (author of Chapter 9) recommended this film because she felt it could provide another point of view to our discussion on literacy, specifically Black gay and lesbian authors. Because we had not talked much about the intersection of race and sexuality in film and literature, the group agreed this might be one resource to highlight the legendary works of famous Black gay artist/writers, such as Baldwin, Hughes, and others.

Fecho, B. (2001). "Why are you doing this?": Acknowledging and transcending threat in a critical inquiry classroom. *Research in the Teaching of English, 36* (1), 9–37.

Through a series of vignettes, drawn from his intensive teacher inquiry project, located in his urban high English classroom, Fecho examines how his use of critical inquiry pedagogy exacerbated threat, but also made space for participants to acknowledge and trascend threat. Together, he and his students (all of whom were either African or Caribbean American) examined issues of culture, race, and ethnicity through various inquiry projects. Many school stakeholders—including Fecho's colleagues, students and their parents, and himself—found that their beliefs and identities were threatened in the course of this work. As Fecho points out, though, threat is always already present in classrooms; inquiry-based pedagogy can provide a space for examining that threat, investigating it, and learning from the process.

For many of the Pink TIGers, Fecho's article was a touchstone text for understanding critical inquiry and our own processes as a teacher inquiry group.

Finnerty, D. (2004). *An open letter to my White lesbian, gay, bisexual, transgender sisters and brothers.* Retrieved January 8, 2009, from http://www.tolerance.org/images/teach/current/Open_Letter.pdf

Finnerty believes that White people, and particularly queer White people, have a responsibility to learn the history of the civil rights struggles of minorities, to understand how the struggle for LGBT civil rights and other minorities' struggles for civil rights—especially African Americans—intersect, and where they differ. She asserts that it is irresponsible to merely borrow sound bites from the civil rights battle of the 1960s without taking into account the history of the issues, which are vastly different. She also believes oppressed people should stand together for the rights of all, rather than struggling for rights at each others' expense.

The TIGers read this text after the 2004 election, in which gay marriage rights were denied. Some of the TIGers who are not people of color had borrowed language from the African American civil rights movement to discuss the homophobia motivating that decision, and we read this article to better understand the role of our White privilege in our struggle for marriage equality.

First Amendment Center Online Staff. (2008, July 29). Federal judge raps Fla. principal for treatment of gay students. *The Associated Press.* Retrieved January 8, 2009, from http://www.firstamendmentcenter.org/news.aspx?id=20351

This brief online summary of the events in the *Gillman v. School Board of Holmes County* case addresses students' rights to free speech. In the case, Principal David Davis of Ponce de Leon High School prohibited students from wearing clothing, buttons, or other symbols that showed support for a lesbian classmate who had been harassed for being gay. Heather Gillman (one of the students who wished to show support by wearing GLBT-friendly symbols) and the American Civil Liberties Union sued the school district, winning a case in which it was ruled that the principal and school board had violated the students' First Amendment rights when prohibiting the peaceful expressions of support.

Fossey, R. (2008, August 18). "I support my gay friends": Free speech is alive and well in the schools of the Florida Panhandle. *Teachers College Record*. Retrieved October 7, 2008, from http://www.tcrecord.org. ID number: 15349.

> In this column, Fossey summarizes, in more detail than the First Amendment Center Online version, the specific events of the *Gillman v. School Board of Holmes County* case and the ruling of Judge Smoak that students possess a constitutional right to freedom of expression in peacefully showing support for classmates. Fossey also discusses how this case fits with other, recent cases in which students have challenged schools' censorship of free speech.
>
> We read this article as the TIGers were preparing to discuss the *Gillman* case, and found it useful to us in considering how we might advocate for students' rights at times such as the "Day of Silence" in which several TIGers' GSAs participate or in advocating for the rights of transgender students to wear clothing appropriate to the gender to which they are transitioning.

Gjestvang, L., & Youth Video OUTreach Collective (Producer & Director). (2007). *20 straws: Growing up gay* [Motion picture]. (Available from http://videooutreach.org/)

> This youth-produced video chronicles the high school experiences of nine out gay and lesbian youth in central Ohio. Created with several teaching artists, including the director, Liv Gjestvang, the film was made in 18 months and highlights the day-to-day experiences, dreams, and setbacks of these young people, including how they came out to family and friends, when they came out, the consequences of their coming out, and how they have been supported (or not) in engaging in school life, including attending the prom and other events.
>
> The Pink TIGers have several connections to this film. Both Mollie (author of Chapter 10) and Lauren (author of Chapter 4) consulted with the filmmakers during production, and all the Pink TIGers attended Central Ohio screenings of the film. Pink TIGers have also screened the film in the courses that they teach and at GSA meetings.

Gunther, J. (Director). (2005, March 22). *Postcards from Buster:* "Sugartime!" [Television broadcast]. Columbus, OH: Public Broadcasting Service.

> In this episode of the PBS children's series *Postcards from Buster*, Buster visits families in Vermont, including a lesbian couple and their children, during the maple sugar season. The episode sparked controversy nationally when the then secretary of education, Margaret Spellings, denounced PBS

for spending money on this episode. Originally, PBS chose not to air the episode in January 2005. However, viewers, including many of the Pink TIGers, wrote letters and phoned local affiliates in protest of that decision. In Columbus, the episode finally aired in early spring as part of a special edition of the PBS local news show *Viewpoint* (in a 7:00 pm time slot) rather than at its usual afternoon time. The *Buster* episode was followed by a discussion among panelists, including the leader of Stonewall Columbus, an early childhood educator, and a former gay man speaking against the program.

The TIGers viewed a recording of the "Sugartime!" episode and the subsequent *Viewpoint* panel discussion at a meeting in May 2005. We discussed how frequently the term "sexualized" was used by the panel despite the fact that the show focused mostly on the process of making maple syrup and sugar and sharing in the process with friends and family. Lauren (author of Chapter 4) and Jill (author of Chapter 8) also showed the episode to their students, or shared newspaper and other media items written about the episode. Their students, likewise, did not see what was controversial in the episode.

hooks, b. (2000). Homophobia in Black communities. In D. Constantine-Simms (Ed.), *The greatest taboo: Homosexuality in Black communities* (pp. 67–73). Los Angeles: Alyson Books.

hooks's writing of this chapter grew out of assumptions in many feminist circles that Black communities are somehow more homophobic than White or other communities in the United States. Although she acknowledges that many Christian African Americans (like many other Christians) believe that homosexuality is a sin, and that some Black communities may be indeed be more homophobic because of the way antigay sentiments are expressed, she argues that the "greatest threat to gay rights does not reside in black communities" (p. 69). Creating an authentic Black community, according to hooks, involves a "vigilant protest of homophobia" by uniting the gay liberation struggle and the Black liberation struggle to resist all forms of domination.

We initially used this text to shed light on the various ways homophobia was expressed in some communities, specifically in Black communities.

Hubbard, R. S., & Power, B. M. (1999). *Living the question: A guide for teacher-researchers*. York, ME: Stenhouse.

This book is premised on the idea that classroom-based action research is a natural extension of good teaching. Hubbard and Power advocate for close observations of students and systematically studying one's own teaching in order to see the patterns in and make sense of practice. They urge teachers to pay attention to the curiosities, complexities, and tensions in their teaching and classrooms, and to use these interests to frame questions for further exploration and research. They also suggest close-to-the-classroom ways for gathering and analyzing data, and suggest broad reading of texts from an array of genres (fiction, nonfiction, and poetry, along with empirical studies) as sources to inform one's research. The book also includes examples and essays from practitioners engaged in research in the "Featured Teacher Researcher" sections.

The TIGers read excerpts from this book at different points across our time together. Sections on finding a research focus and framing questions for inquiry were useful as we started our work together. We also read sections on analyzing data and writing up research in preparation for our writing retreat.

Kilman, C. (2007, Spring). "This is why we need a GSA." *Teaching Tolerance,* 30–37.

Kilman uses Gay, Lesbian, and Straight Education Network (GLSEN) statistics as well as anecdotal evidence from teachers and students in Madison, Wisconsin, to support the need for GSAs in middle schools. Although most of the TIGers have experience solely with secondary rather than middle school GSAs, we all empathize with the frustrations of not having enough control over making school spaces safer for our students. This is an article that every middle and high school teacher and administrator should read and make visible on a bulletin board somewhere in the school.

Kosciw, J. G., Diaz, E. M., & Greytak, E. A. (2008). *The 2007 National School Climate Survey: The experiences of lesbian, gay, bisexual, and transgender youth in our nation's schools.* New York: GLSEN.

The 2007 National School Climate Survey draws on more than 6,000 LGBT students from all 50 states regarding bullying, harassing language, staff and school involvement, and policy measures in schools. The findings reinforce the need for more work in creating safer schools and inclusive policies for schools.

This survey, as well as the earlier versions of it, reminded us of the importance of our efforts and gave us something to point to in explaining the significance of our work to others. Interestingly, the surveys, across time, like our group, have become more attentive to intersecting identities, such as race, class, gender, and sexuality, and more attentive to the unique situation of transgender students.

Lee, A. (Director), Proulx, A., & McMurtry, L. (Authors). (2005). *Brokeback mountain*. [Motion picture]. United States: Universal Studios.

> Based on Annie Proulx's beautiful yet tragic story of two young men who fall in love while herding sheep in rural Wyoming in the early 1960s, this film depicts a gay couple's relationship as well as its deterioration at the hand of the limitations of traditional social conventions. This film is rated R, but excerpts would be appropriate for high school students, particularly if used in conjunction with nonfiction accounts of violence against GLBTQ individuals such as Lawrence King or Harvey Milk. With high school students, teachers might consider a full reading of Proulx's story as a primary text for increased accessibility to the themes covered in the film.

Miller, R. E. (2000). Fault lines in the contact zone: Assessing homophobic student writing. In W. J. Spurlin (Ed.), *Lesbian and gay studies and the teaching of English: Positions, pedagogies, and cultural politics* (pp. 234–252). Urbana, IL: National Council of Teachers of English.

> Miller's essay takes up Mary Louise Pratt's idea of classrooms as "contact zones" and considers what becomes of unsolicited oppositional discourse, particularly as it surfaces in student writing. He contends that teachers should not simply tell students, "No language that is racist, sexist, homophobic, or that degrades the working class will be allowed in our discussion" (p. 250). Rather, he suggests that the way to truly engage in the contact zone is to "closely attend to what our students say and write in an ongoing effort to learn how to read, understand, and respond to the strange, sometimes threatening, multivocal texts they produce while writing in the contact zone" (pp. 251–252).
>
> For the TIGers, Miller's essay was provocative, forcing us to consider how (and whether) to engage with the hateful ideas that our students might raise through their talk and writing. We saw value in the concept of the "contact zone," and wondered, together, how to achieve this kind of space while also working to create the kinds of "safe" spaces we envisioned for young people in schools.

Mills, G. E. (2006). *Action research: A guide for the teacher researcher* (3rd ed.). Upper Saddle River, NJ: Merrill Prentice Hall.

> Like Hubbard & Power (1999), this book provides a basic overview for engaging in action research in classroom-based contexts. Structured as more of a textbook, this volume moves systematically, chapter by chapter, through the action research process. Again, the TIGers read excerpts from the book, including sections on framing research questions and approaches to ethical issues in research.

Mitchell, C. (2000). "What's out there?" Gay and lesbian literature for children and young adults. In W. J. Spurlin (Ed.), *Lesbian and gay studies and the teaching of English: Positions, pedagogies, and cultural politics* (pp. 112–130). Urbana, IL: National Council of Teachers of English.

Mitchell prompts teachers to ask what they are hoping to accomplish by sharing GLBT literature with children and young adults. She suggests that teachers might consider the different kinds of narratives offered by the literature currently available—narratives that reflect the richness and diversity of experiences of GLBT people but also narratives that are targeted at helping the heterosexual community better reconsider their own sexuality as constructed. Offering multiple, specific examples of texts for children and young adults, Mitchell discusses what these texts might offer teachers and youth.

The TIGers purchased copies of two of the texts reviewed in this chapter (*Am I Blue?* and *Asha's Mums*) to be given to participating teachers when we screened *It's Elementary* and *It's Still Elementary* in October 2008.

Moje, E. B., & MuQaribu, M. (2003). Literacy and sexual identity. *Journal of Adolescent and Adult Literacy, 47*(3), 204–208.

This brief "first person" account is coauthored by a teacher educator and a preservice teacher. In it, they argue that sexual identity matters in literacy education because literacy learning is influenced by the connections learners are able to make between literacy and their life experiences, which include sexuality. They assert that we need more research in this arena to better prepare teachers to address issues related to sexual identity in their classes.

Our group—and our individual and collective projects—is one response to their call. This article was distributed to group members early in our 1st year of meeting as a way of positioning ourselves as researchers who had something important and specific to contribute to our fields.

Newman, L. (1988). A letter to Harvey Milk. *A letter to Harvey Milk: Short stories* (pp. 25–28). Ithaca, NY: Firebrand Books.

In this moving short story, Harry, an elderly Jewish man, takes a writing class at a senior center in San Francisco. For his first writing assignment, he writes a letter to his friend, the late Harvey Milk, the first openly gay U.S. elected official (a member of the San Francisco Board of Supervisors). He sees a pink triangle on the teacher's backpack, which brings back memories of concentration camps for Harry, and upon being asked to write a story he's never told anyone, he writes about his friend Izzy's relationship with another man in a concentration camp.

Lauren (author of Chapter 4) and Jason (author of Chapter 5) mentioned that they used the text in their classrooms. Other TIGers used the text in their high school classrooms as well.

Osborne, K. L. (2000). "Swimming upstream": Recovering the lesbian in Native American literature. In W. J. Spurlin (Ed.), *Lesbian and gay studies and the teaching of English: Positions, pedagogies, and cultural politics* (pp. 191–210). Urbana, IL: National Council of Teachers of English.

In this chapter the author argues that Native American literature has largely been appropriated by non–Native Americans, which has served to reduce and essentialize Native Americans—especially with regard to portrayals of gay and lesbian figures. Osborne gives a detailed summary and interpretation of stories by Native American author Beth Brant as examples of narratives that can reveal complex individuals within the specific identity of a lesbian Native American. She argues that texts like these that complicate identities are critical contributions to a meaningful multicultural education.

After reading this chapter, the Pink TIGers decided to purchase, read, and discuss Brant's *Food and Spirits*. (See earlier annotation.)

Reese, J. (2000). Creating a place for lesbian and gay readings in secondary English classrooms. In W. J. Spurlin (Ed.), *Lesbian and gay studies and the teaching of English: Positions, pedagogies, and cultural politics* (pp. 131–146). Urbana, IL: National Council of Teachers of English.

Jim Reese, a teacher who self-identifies as gay, shares his interpretation of reading the film *Strictly Ballroom* as a gay text, then connects this reading with Rosenblatt's reader response theory. Specifically, for example, he echoes Rosenblatt's assertion that readers should be encouraged by teachers to authentically locate themselves in texts. Reese challenges teacher reluctance to allow gay and lesbian students this opportunity, noting that limiting visibility of gay and lesbian readings inhibits imagined identities for gay and lesbian students. For Reese, the discovery of his own gay reading of *Strictly Ballroom* has inspired him to live his life more fully and has led him to advocate for more inclusive readings for all students. Reese's chapter would be helpful for teachers or teacher educators who are interested in creating and maintaining a more equitable classroom.

Reese's chapter provided a springboard for the Pink TIGers to discuss LGBT-inclusive texts and helped us understand how to engage in gay readings of a broad array of texts that many of us teach or have taught in our own classrooms, including works by Shakespeare and other canonical works.

Reeves, K. E. (1999). All God's children. *Essence, 30*(7), 220.

This brief essay was written by a "churchgoing Black Christian" who is also a gay man and a political activist. He writes about his church member-ship of more than 25 years; his partner of 30 years; and his years in public service, including as a City Council member and, later, a mayor. He writes about the ways that his various identities have come into conflict with one another over the years, particularly how various sermons have negatively positioned him as a gay man, and how, as an activist, he has challenged such positioning. Ultimately, he argues that Black gays and lesbians de-serve recognition and respect from their Black faith communities.

Mollie (author of Chapter 10) brought this essay to the group very early in our 1st year of meeting as a way of adding to our discussion about intersections of racial and sexual identities and as an attempt to alleviate pressure on Anette (author of Chapter 9), as the only person of color in the group, to speak for all people of color.

Reis, B. (2008, fall). Making sense of the senseless: The murder of Lawrence King. *Teaching Tolerance, 34.* Retrieved January 8, 2009, from http://www.tolerance.org/teach/magazine/features.jsp?p=0&is=43&ar=943

In this article, Reis poses the question: "Should adults encourage LGBT youth to come out?" Reis explains that some people feel that the adults, who supposedly encouraged Lawrence King to come out, could be, at least in part, to blame for King's murder. The article looks at the pros and cons of coming out as a teen or waiting until one is a bit older.

This piece was discussed during two different Pink TIGer meetings. Members shared their overall thoughts about the article and debated what it meant to "encourage" someone to come or be out.

Setoodeh, R. (2008, July 19). Young, gay, and murdered. *Newsweek.* Retrieved June 18, 2009, from http://www.newsweek.com/id/147790

Lawrence King, a 15-year-old gay student, was shot in the head in school by a homophobic classmate. The article frames King's murder as the end result of a series of events where, in part, students, school staff, and King's foster parents fall victim to his outrageous demands and expressions of sexuality.

As TIGers, we were devastated by the news of King's death and, over-all, had mixed feelings about the way that some of the views expressed in the article were presented. We felt, for example, that the assistant principal who counseled King was portrayed in an unfair manner. One of the posi-tive uses we found for the article was that it helped us to facilitate discus-sions about how we could better support students who are out or intend to come out to us, or come out more generally, in our schools.

Talburt, S. (2000). On not coming out; Or, Reimagining limits. In W. J. Spurlin (Ed.), *Lesbian and gay studies and the teaching of English: Positions, pedagogies, and cultural politics* (pp. 54–78). Urbana, IL: National Council of Teachers of English.

In this chapter Talburt explores what it means to resist the integration of one's sexual identity with one's academic and pedagogical work. Talburt shares the story of "Olivia." An associate professor of English, Olivia works to destabilize and unfix her identity in her classes so that she is not limited to speaking for a group or from a static category of identification. By not coming out to her students, Olivia resists being taken up as a "text" in her class, instead creating situations "in which she and her students must enact positions in relation to the texts under study" (p. 58).

Talburt's chapter held significance for many of the TIGers. Several of us questioned the viability of a teacher's not being taken up as a text in the classroom. Talburt's chapter pushed all of us to think seriously about the relationships between identity, pedagogy, and our political commitments as educators.

About the Contributors

Mollie V. Blackburn is an Associate Professor in the School of Teaching and Learning at The Ohio State University. Her most recent research projects include the teacher inquiry project described in this book and a book discussion group with Pink TIGers' students who come together to read and discuss LGBT-themed young adult literature. She has also studied the ways local LGBTQ youth experience gender rules and regulations in schools. In her dissertation research, she focused on the ways LGBTQ youth used literacies and language to work for social change in and beyond schools. Her scholarship received the Ralph C. Preston Award for dissertations that work for social justice and the Alan C. Purves Award for articles in *Research in the Teaching of English* that are deemed rich with classroom implications.

Caroline T. Clark is an Associate Professor in the School of Teaching and Learning in the College of Education and Human Ecology at The Ohio State University. Her scholarship focuses on adolescents' literacy practices across formal/school and informal settings and community-based literacy research with young people for social action. Her commitments to literacy research as a means for political action and social justice shape her scholarship and teaching. Most recently she has worked with Mollie Blackburn to facilitate and document the work of a book discussion group with high school students who meet to discuss LGBT-themed literature.

Jeane F. Copenhaver-Johnson is an Associate Professor of Education at The Ohio State University at Mansfield, where she teaches courses in language, literacy, and multicultural education. Her scholarship and teaching encourage critical reconsideration of sociological processes by which social inequities are sustained and reproduced, particularly in schools and classrooms. She also has been transforming this philosophy into a pedagogy of action, now shared by former students creating anti-homophobic/antiheterosexist experiences and environments in their own schools. Jeane shares her life with her partner, Lynn Johnson; daughter, Alison; and three furry pets.

Jason Gonzales has been a working musician, a recording engineer, and a teacher and is now a media designer/web developer. As a teacher he was motivated to pursue social justice through activism and teaching students how to create their own digital media. He has helped train other teachers how to use digital media production in their teaching and wrote his master's thesis about digital media and new literacies based on classroom research. He earned his MA in English education from The Ohio State University. Jason still volunteers his services toward causes of social justice and public service as a media designer.

Mindy Hall graduated from The Ohio State University with a BS in education and received an M.Ed. in curriculum and instruction from Ashland University. During her 20 years as an educator she has taught Grades 1, 2, and 3. Currently she teaches 2nd-grade language arts at Maryland Elementary School in Bexley, Ohio. Additionally, she is the district's international/multicultural education coordinator and the president of her local teaching association. Mindy joined the Pink TIGers to learn about current elementary and secondary LGBTQ resources, to find ways to incorporate LGBTQ issues into the curriculum, and to collaborate with educators in different school districts and at the university level.

Lauren M. Kenney received an M.Ed. from The Ohio State University. She has been teaching 9th- and 10th-grade English at the Arts and College Preparatory Academy for the past 6 years and has used her identity as an out lesbian, her position as GSA advisor, literature, and film to fight homophobia and transphobia in her classroom and schoolwide. She lives with her partner, Kelly, and their son, Gus, in Bellingham, Washington. Please visit her, TIGers.

Anette Melvin received her undergraduate and master's degrees from the University of Dayton. She has worked in urban settings for more than 11 years and taught pre-K through 5th grade before deciding to pursue other interests. Currently, she is completing her PhD in early childhood education at The Ohio State University. Her focus is on issues of equity and diversity in education, with an emphasis on identity and its impact on teaching and learning. She lives in Columbus, Ohio, with her two cats—Toffee and Piérre.

Ryan Schey is starting his 2nd year teaching at Delaware Hayes High School and has recently completed his Master of Education degree in English education at The Ohio State University. He teaches American literature and broadcast journalism along with a team-taught humanities course. His teaching passions include integrating social justice, using graphic novels, and incorporating technology and media literacy into his classes. Outside the classroom, Ryan coadvises the school's gay-straight alliance and works on the district's multicultural committee to cultivate a greater understanding of diversity in his community. His teaching has led him to work with national organizations such as the National Council of Teachers of English and the Student Television Network. He currently resides with his partner in Lewis Center, Ohio.

Jill M. Smith is a doctoral candidate in the School of Teaching and Learning at The Ohio State University and teaches high school English classes in Westerville, Ohio. She is the GSA advisor at Westerville Central High School and serves on her district's antiharassment committee as well as its curriculum council. As a member of the Pink TIGers, she has presented her work at national conferences such as NCTE and AERA. She and her husband, David, live in Olde Towne East, Ohio, with their two dogs.

Ariel Uppstrom is a 2nd-year English teacher and a graduate of The Ohio State University Master of Education program. She works with 10th- and 12th-grade students, focusing on social justice and expanding their exposure to global ideas. Besides her classroom endeavors, she participates in the district's multicultural committee, which focuses on building an inclusive atmosphere in the district. Ariel belongs to a number of professional teaching organizations and hopes to present at NCTE in the future. She enjoys traveling and hopes to move to a Spanish-speaking country to begin her positive work beyond borders. Ariel currently resides in Worthington, Ohio, with her partner and their two cats.

Index